APPREHENDING FLEEING SUSPECTS

APPREHENDING FLEEING SUSPECTS

Suspect Tactics and Perimeter Control

By

JACK H. SCHONELY

CHARLES C THOMAS • PUBLISHER, LTD.
Springfield • Illinois • U.S.A.

Published and Distributed Throughout the World by

CHARLES C THOMAS • PUBLISHER, LTD.
2600 South First Street
Springfield, Illinois 62704

©2005 by CHARLES C THOMAS • PUBLISHER, LTD.

ISBN 0-398-07541-7

Library of Congress Catalog Card Number: 2004053675

With THOMAS BOOKS *careful attention is given to all details of man-
ufacturing and design. It is the Publisher's desire to present books that are sat-
isfactory as to their physical qualities and artistic possibilities and appropriate for their particular use.* THOMAS BOOKS *will be true to those laws
of quality that assure a good name and good will.*

Printed in the United States of America
CR-R-3

Library of Congress Cataloging-in-Publication Data

Schonely, Jack H.
    Apprehending fleeing suspects : suspect tactics and perimeter
containment / by Jack H. Schonely.
        p. cm.
    Includes index.
    ISBN 0-398-07541-7 (pbk.)
    1. Arrest (Police methods) 2. Fugitives from justice. I. Title.

HV8080.A6S34 2004
363.2'32--dc22
                                                                2004053675

FOREWORD

Law enforcement is a dangerous profession interspersed with tactical challenges, adrenalin flow, teamwork and ultimately, the apprehension of criminals. There is nothing more satisfying for a police officer than to observe suspicious activity, investigate it and end up in a vehicle and/or foot pursuit where the suspect is safely apprehended. Apprehending fleeing suspects is one of the most difficult aspects of our profession. In this book, Jack Schonely addresses the basics of how to safely capture suspects who attempt to flee from the police.

During the reader's review, one will quickly realize that Jack is a seasoned and highly competent police officer whose intent is to clearly offer his experiences as a template for police officers from the smallest to the largest of departments to consider when faced with a situation involving, "fleeing suspects." His focus is on whether to chase or contain, how to set up perimeters, management of the incident, physical conditioning, use of airborne resources, canines, communications, tactical deployment, training, suspect tactics, and most importantly incident debriefing techniques.

This book is one of the most comprehensive and "to the point" manuscripts that I have had the pleasure to review in my 38 years of law enforcement. *Apprehending Fleeing Suspects* is the how to, nuts and bolts of field enforcement tactics and is not only focused on "suspect apprehension," but on officer safety. A must read for the professional police officer.

MIKE HILLMANN, DEPUTY CHIEF
Special Operations Bureau
Los Angeles Police Department

PREFACE

The training of law enforcement officers has changed dramatically over the past 30 years. New policing techniques and technology have law enforcement agencies of all sizes changing how they do business on a daily basis. The officers of today receive training on modern equipment that existed only in the imaginations of their predecessors. Some of the training relates to officer tactics and survival and recently a great deal of emphasis has been directed towards vehicle pursuits. One particular area of police work gets little or no attention in the training realm, how to successfully and safely apprehend a fleeing suspect on foot.

Most officers learn about foot pursuits by being in foot pursuit. On-the-job training or "OJT" has been the technique used to teach young officers how to handle this inevitable event. Officers learn through trial and error as to what works and what doesn't. In the meantime many of the criminals being chased easily get away. Unfortunately, some of these criminals are extremely dangerous individuals who must be captured for public safety.

There are excellent containment techniques that have proven success. These techniques are available to every law enforcement officer fighting crime. The success or failure of this tool depends on training and knowledge prior to the foot pursuit ever taking place. Not only must the officer in foot pursuit have this knowledge, but all of the officers responding to assist the primary officer must possess the same information. This technique truly requires a team effort from start to finish.

As important as learning and understanding "perimeter containment" techniques, is understanding what criminals will do to avoid capture. The criminal element has learned how law enforcement operates and has updated the tactics they use to evade us. These tactics are constantly changing, but certain trends are very evident.

This book will introduce the reader to "perimeter containment" as a technique in apprehending a fleeing suspect on foot. It will also provide information on the tactics being used by criminals to avoid capture, working with airborne law enforcement, and K-9 search operations.

Whether this technique is used nightly, weekly, a couple times a year, or once in a career, it is vital to be prepared before the event occurs. This knowledge, along with training and practice, gives the advantage to the officer, particularly during critical incidents where the capture of the suspect is paramount.

J.H.S.

ACKNOWLEDGMENTS

I have had the privilege of working with so many outstanding police officers in the past twenty-four years. I have learned much of the information shared in this book working the streets in a patrol car with many of those officers. I am grateful for their tactical knowledge, street smarts, and their friendship. I am particularly grateful to the men and women of the Los Angeles Police Department's 77th Street Division to whom I owe so much. 77th Street is where I learned to be a street cop on the "morning watch" and where I first learned about how to capture a fleeing suspect.

I am also thankful to have worked with a small group of courageous officers in Metropolitan Division K-9. Thanks to all I worked with during those five exciting years, so much of this book's roots started during those perimeter searches for the most dangerous felons Los Angeles had to offer. A special thanks to Danny Bunch and Jim Hagerty for their friendship and shared passion on the subject of perimeter containment.

The information from this book was fine-tuned by working with so many outstanding officers at Air Support Division. Thanks to all of you for the countless scenarios shared with me as you fought crime from the air.

Thanks to Patrick McNamara, Kris Owen, Bruce Hunt, Bob Green, Rick Lawin, Mike Grossman, Leslie Judge, Chris Warren, and Jim Weigh for their unique skills, never-ending support, honest opinions, and most of all their friendship.

Many thanks to Deputy Chief Mike Hillmann for contributing the foreword to this book. His leadership and tactical knowledge are appreciated by all of us in the LAPD.

Glenn Grossman and Los Angeles Daily News photographer Hans Gutknecht contributed the photographs for the book. They are both very talented photographers and I am fortunate to feature their work in the pages to follow and even more fortunate to call them friends.

A special thanks to my entire family for their unwavering support of all that I do. I am forever grateful for having an incredible wife and children. Tracy, Ian, and Megan, I love you.

CONTENTS

APPREHENDING FLEEING SUSPECTS

Chapter 1

FOOT PURSUIT VS. CONTAINMENT

Foot pursuits of criminals can be one of the most hazardous situations that an officer can encounter. They are extremely unpredictable and contain many challenges and hazards in addition to the suspect. Many officers over the years have found themselves chasing a suspect through a back yard only to find themselves flat on their backs seconds later from an unseen clothesline. The list of hazards is endless particularly during hours of darkness. The unseen clothesline could just as easily be the unseen pit bull, open trench, barbed wire fence, or empty swimming pool. Officers have received serious injuries from hazards such as these as the suspect runs off into the darkness.

Every foot pursuit is unique, but every officer must be realistic when evaluating the situation. During foot pursuits many tactical decisions are made quickly by the officer. One of those decisions will be whether to continue to chase or attempt to contain the suspect. Some of the factors involved in this decision are listed below.

- Age of the suspect.
- Nature of the crime.
- Is the suspect known to be armed?
- Location of the foot pursuit.
- Time of day.
- Physical fitness of the officer.
- Available resources.
- Number of suspects.

AGE OF THE SUSPECT

Many suspects are younger than even most rookie officers on the street. This is significant for obvious reasons, speed and fitness. A quick look at a suspect as he bails out of a vehicle will make it clear to the officer what kind of effort is going to be required to chase, catch, and handcuff the suspect. Evaluating the suspect and yourself at the same time is a must for officer safety in this situation. What are the realistic chances of my chasing down this suspect?

NATURE OF THE CRIME

This factor is not always clear to the pursuing officer. Most officers have experienced capturing a shoplifter only to find out hours later that the suspect is wanted for a more serious offense in another jurisdiction. Because this is such a common occurrence in law enforcement, officers should be on guard and use extreme caution during every foot pursuit. Rarely, do you know *exactly* what you have in front of you.

If the crime is known at the time of the chase, it should be evaluated from not only an officer safety perspective, but overall public safety perspective as well. Did this suspect attempt to steal a car or did the suspect shoot someone? The suspect's actions and desperation will certainly be different for these two crimes and the risk to you and the public are different as well. Containment is oftentimes the better choice with a more serious crime.

IS THE SUSPECT KNOWN TO BE ARMED?

This factor can have several forms. One is that the officer pursuing observes a weapon on the suspect as the foot pursuit ensues. Second, was a weapon used during the commission of the crime as reported by a victim? Third, is the suspect known to the officer and has that suspect been armed in the past? All of these possibilities put officer safety at risk and must be part of the decision process on "foot pursuit vs. containment." All foot pursuits have some risk involved. A foot pursuit of an armed suspect is dangerous and should be avoided if at all possible. There are certainly times when we in law enforcement are required to take risks to complete our duties. If given a choice between entering a dark rear yard where a suspect with a gun just turned the corner or setting a containment, the containment is in most cases the best choice.

Treating all suspects during a foot pursuit as if they were armed is a good practice. During the foot pursuit the suspects' actions should be watched carefully. If the suspect is reaching for or holding their waistband, officers should consider this when deciding to continue to pursue or contain. Extreme caution should be used at every turn and every obstacle.

LOCATION OF THE FOOT PURSUIT

How familiar with the area is the officer who is in foot pursuit? This can be important when it comes to those hazards discussed earlier. You can be sure that if the suspect has chosen this location to bail out and run that *he* knows what hazards are ahead. Most jurisdictions have "problem locations" that are well known to officers. If the suspect is running in one of those areas, the officer should consider that as an increased risk of continuing to pursue.

During vehicle pursuits, how the pursuit terminates is a factor to consider with regards to location. Did the suspect choose to bail out at a particular location or did he crash his vehicle? Suspects who choose to bail out tend to be very familiar with where they are about to run. Officers should take that into consideration and evaluate the risk.

A second part of the location factor is this. Are you running down a sidewalk or are you going into rear yards hopping fences? These are two very different locations with regards to the risk to the officer. Even if the officer decides to contain rather than pursue, it is often a good idea to chase and keep the suspect in sight as long as possible and then contain when the suspect turns into the houses. The risk is minimal running down a sidewalk and knowing exactly where the suspect turns into the houses will benefit the containment later.

TIME OF DAY

This is a simple concept; darkness increases the risk of *all* of these factors and must be considered tactically.

PHYSICAL FITNESS OF THE OFFICER

This factor is seldom discussed but could be the difference between success and failure and more importantly life or death. Knowing your personal limitations is the key. An officer who stays in good physical condition not only has a better chance of catching the suspect, but is also better prepared for an altercation that could ensue. It is one thing to chase a suspect for two blocks and catch him; it is another to have to fight him for several minutes after the chase to get the handcuffs on. Are you physically prepared for that scenario? If you choose to chase rather than contain, consider the consequences.

AVAILABLE RESOURCES

This factor can in some ways be one of the most important in determining whether to chase or contain. Resources vary greatly from agency to agency. Many metropolitan police departments have large numbers of officers on patrol at any given time and some have aviation units quickly responding to assist. Response to an officer in foot pursuit will be swift and decisive. Other agencies are spread very thin where the nearest back-up is ten minutes or more away.

Every officer must have a realistic assessment of how long it will take for the first backing officer to arrive on scene. An officer who knows that the response will be very fast has a little more discretion in choosing to chase or contain. It is certainly a more difficult decision for the officer who knows that help is on the way, but that it will take some time to respond. The risk is greater for that officer. Thousands of brave officers deal with that reality every day when they put on the badge.

Available resources with a reasonable estimated time of arrival play a significant role when containing an area. This will become more evident later, but for now it is important to know that this factor must be considered in realistic terms when making tactical and officer safety decisions. Officer safety should always be a primary concern, capturing the suspect is second.

NUMBER OF SUSPECTS

This should be common sense but is certainly worth mentioning. Going in foot pursuit of multiple suspects with only one officer should be avoided. The officer should attempt to keep the suspects in sight from a safe distance and set perimeter containment when the opportunity arises.

All of these factors must be evaluated in seconds while chasing the suspect. It is a lot to think about in a short amount of time. It is vital to think about these factors ahead of time, talk about them with fellow officers, and train for these inevitable scenarios. Thus, the factors will become second nature and the tactical decision-making process will be smooth and fast. Be prepared, have a plan, execute the plan.

COMMUNICATION

Even with all of this going on, we haven't even talked about communication. A clear and concise radio broadcast is oftentimes the key to a successful foot pursuit and or perimeter containment. This is always challenging for officers. The heart is pumping, adrenaline is flowing, and the respiratory rate is through the roof. Now, should we expect the officer to make a clear radio broadcast? Absolutely, it's a must. This is the only way any help is going to get to where they need it.

The location is the priority. Even if nothing else gets out, *the location is vital.* Without that, all the help in the world is meaningless. But don't settle on that because success and safety are going to be determined by the information broadcasted over the radio. The fact that an officer is in foot pursuit followed by the location and direction of travel is a great start to success. An example of a concise first broadcast might look something like this.

"Unit One is in foot pursuit, Westbound Oak Street approaching Main."

Many times officers try to say too much when only basic information is required. What information does the officer responding need to know to assist the officer in foot pursuit? A description of the suspect is secondary to location and direction of travel. Keeping it simple is best. This also allows the officer to breathe between broadcasts. A long drawn-out broadcast with too much information takes a lot of air and usually becomes unreadable by the end. Short updates of the location are good and when able a very basic description of the suspect will be helpful. Basic is the key word. Sex, race, and clothing are the vitals. Descriptors like height, weight, hair, and tattoos are a waste of breath unless they are extremely unique. An example might be a suspect who is very tall. These descriptors will be important later, but on the initial broadcasts only the basics are best.

"Suspect male white, white shirt, blue jeans, still Westbound."

I cannot overemphasize the importance of a *clear and concise initial broadcast.* This broadcast will often set the tone for the rest of the incident and can determine the outcome.

Chapter 2

DECISION TO CONTAIN

B efore making the decision to contain, officers must fully understand what perimeter containment is and what is required for success.

"PERIMETER CONTAINMENT" is the containment of an area, large or small, utilizing officers deployed to the corners, with a clear line of sight of ALL sides of that containment area.

The simple goal of perimeter containment is to limit the movement of a fleeing suspect in an area that officers control using themselves and their police vehicles as a visible deterrent to the suspect. That area whether it is a single residence, an entire block, four blocks, or a rural wooded area can then be searched systematically for the suspect.

Officers either visible or "perceived" by the suspect fleeing are the wall that contains them inside an area, i.e., an empty patrol car at a corner to deter suspects from crossing the street. This is certainly not always the case as some suspects will run right past officers in an attempt to escape. But part of the goal of a containment is being able to observe those actions by a suspect and continue to pursue them. During this stage of the process, officers must be thinking about containment versus capture to be most effective.

All sides of a containment area must be clearly observed by officers in order to have success. The more officers sur-

11

rounding an area the easier it is on the individual officer and it is certainly more of a deterrent to the suspect to move.

Using the example of a single block perimeter containment, it can be held by a minimum of two officers diagonally deployed on the block (see Figure 1). This requires both officers to divide their attention to two sides of the block. In some cases the distance could be significant. If two additional officers arrive and take positions on the remaining two corners of the containment, the area that each officer is responsible to observe is cut in half and the deterrence to the suspect increases significantly (see Figure 2). If additional resources are available, they should take positions mid-block on the long side of the block (see Figure 3).

This procedure pertains to containments of all sizes, although the responsibility to officers is greater and more difficult to observe for larger perimeters.

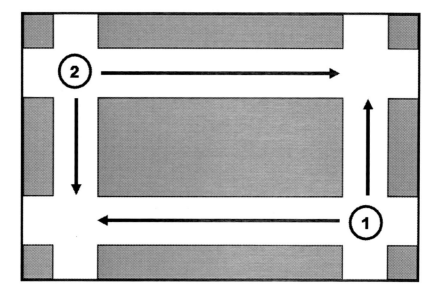

Figure 1. Two officers are able to contain an entire block providing that they are diagonally deployed and able to view all four sides. Their attention must be divided until additional officers arrive to the scene.

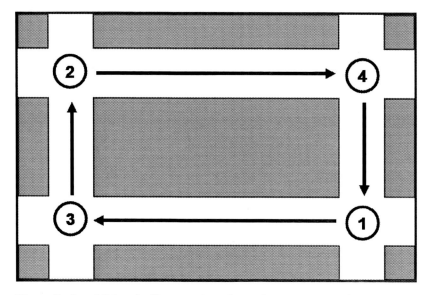

Figure 2: As additional officers arrive, they take positions at the remaining two corners of the containment area. This impacts both the workload and responsibility of the first two officers as well as an added deterrence to the suspect.

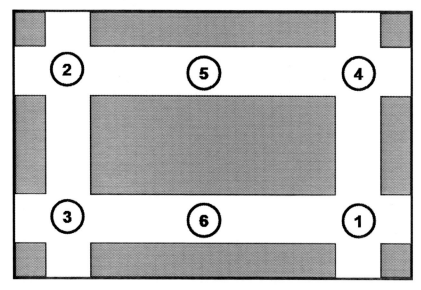

Figure 3. If additional officers are available they should take positions mid-block. Again this will reduce the responsibilities of the first four officers and deter the suspect from "bolting out" in the middle of the block. Placing officers at a mid-block position is particularly important when the containment area is large.

DECISION TO CONTAIN

The timing of the decision to contain is an important element in the ultimate success of the situation. Understanding that most of these situations are extremely fluid and vary greatly, an early and decisive decision to set a perimeter containment will give a greater advantage to the officer.

After the officer has evaluated all of the factors discussed earlier, an educated decision to contain rather than chase can now be made. In some instances this decision can be made prior to the suspect fleeing on foot. For example, during a vehicle pursuit an officer may have a great deal of the information to evaluate all of the factors. Based on those factors an officer may choose to contain the suspect if and when the suspect bails out of the vehicle and runs.

Using the same example of the vehicle pursuit, the primary officer can make a decision to contain before the suspect bails out and communicate the intention to contain to fellow officers involved in the pursuit. This allows all officers involved with the pursuit to prepare themselves for a containment situation rather than a foot pursuit at the termination of the pursuit. Communication and then positioning at the termination point are the keys to success. The advantage is definitely in the favor of the officers in this scenario providing that they all have been trained in how to contain a fleeing suspect.

The primary officer must make a firm decision and clearly communicate that decision to fellow officers for this tactic to work. The backing officers must then trust in that decision and respond to cut off the path of the suspect (see Figure 4). A very common error by officers is to respond to the location where the primary officer last saw the suspect running and not a block or two away in the direction the suspect was running. There is one place that we know the suspect is not, and that is standing next to the primary officer. Yet we often observe three or four patrol cars parked right there and no

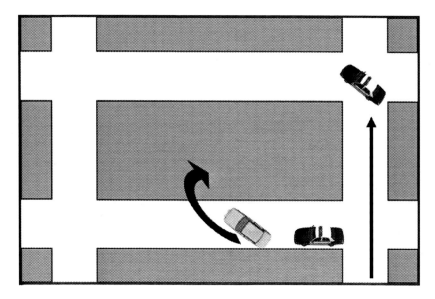

Figure 4. As the suspect bails out of his vehicle and begins running into the block, the second unit must think ahead of the suspect and cut off his path. This quickly contains three sides of the block with the primary officer holding his or her ground.

one thinking ahead of the suspect. Containment needs to be completed as quickly as possible.

The primary officer evaluates the situation, makes a decision to contain, and then communicates the decision to request a "perimeter containment." What does the primary officer need to do next? This will vary depending on the specific situation, but the general rule is to take a position at a corner and continue to communicate pertinent information. If the officer is standing mid-block when they make the decision to contain, they need to move quickly to the nearest corner that best cuts off the path of the suspect's last known direction of travel (see Figure 5). This position allows the officer to cover two sides of the block until additional units arrive on scene.

A feeling of helplessness often occurs at this point. The officer is just standing at a corner waiting for responding

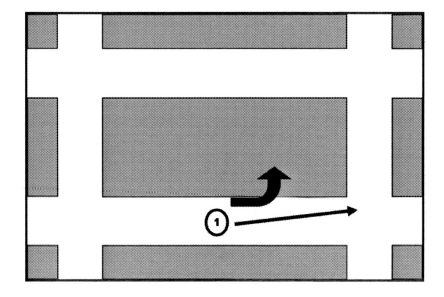

Figure 5: When a suspect turns into a block and the primary officers makes a decision to contain, that officer must quickly move to the nearest corner in order to cover two sides of the block until additional officers arrive. If the officer stands mid-block they only cover one side of the containment area which gives a distinct advantage to the fleeing suspect.

units to arrive, all the time knowing that the suspect is probably still moving. But there are some things that this officer needs to consider.

Finding some cover or concealment should be high on the list. Suspects often come back into view and can pose a threat to the officer particularly if they are armed. Finding a position of cover that allows the officer to still have a clear view of the two sides of the block they are covering is a must.

SIZE OF THE PERIMETER

Another consideration is how large of a perimeter containment to request. The primary officer will be in the best position to make this call based on all of the facts. Some of the same factors discussed earlier come into play on this decision as well. The two main factors are the nature of the crime and estimated time of arrival of assisting officers.

Is the suspect you are chasing wanted for shoplifting or murder? Size of containment should go hand-in-hand with the seriousness of the crime. How bad do you want this suspect? How desperate is the suspect?

Seriousness of the crime, desperation, and how badly you want to capture the suspect tend to parallel each other in the majority of cases. For example, a suspect who just shot a police officer. That is one of the most serious offenses there is, that is the most desperate suspect you will come across, and there is no suspect that we want to capture more than this one. This perimeter containment should be as large as reasonably possible.

It is extremely frustrating to arrive at a scene of an "officer down" and find out that the containment area is one square block with no solid facts to place the suspect inside that area. In the majority of those cases the suspect will not be located inside that area. This should not be a surprise to any experienced law enforcement officer. If you just shot a police officer, are you going to stay in the immediate area waiting for K-9 or SWAT to come and get you? In most cases the answer is a definitive NO. You are going to get as far away as possible in the shortest amount of time possible.

Placing yourself in the offender's shoes for a second will assist the primary officer in determining how large of a containment is needed. Officers can always make the containment area smaller as new facts emerge, but it is extremely difficult to make a containment larger after significant time has passed and have success. Most large perimeter containments do get smaller as time passes. Many factors can contribute to this, including citizen tips of the suspect's location and personal information about the suspect.

During these critical incidents it is important to remember this simple rule:

Do not ASSUME that a suspect is in a particular location without SOLID FACTS to back it up.

Let's use an attempted murder of a police officer scenario. The suspect shoots at the officer and runs into the front door of a residence. There is no further visual contact with the suspect. The primary officer *could* assume that the suspect in now inside and set the containment on just the residence. But there are no solid facts to back up that assumption.

A large perimeter containment should be requested. Once the containment is set, officers can concentrate on the residence first. The containment area allows something to fall back on if the residence is cleared and the suspect is not located. The suspect could have easily gone right out the back door and continued running.

ETA OF ASSISTING OFFICERS

This factor should be secondary to the crime but must be considered. The primary officer must be realistic with regards to how many officers are coming to assist and how long will it take them to arrive. If the ETA is a significant amount of time, a larger perimeter containment may be required. The reason for this should be obvious; the suspect can continue to move while waiting for back-up.

Large perimeters can use up significant resources. Most agencies are not going to commit large numbers of officers to contain and search for a minor offense. On the other hand, the vast majority of agencies will pull out all the stops for a very serious crime particularly when an officer is the victim of that crime. The officer requesting the perimeter containment must consider this factor and make a reasonable request in the size of the containment.

TWO-OFFICER CONTAINMENTS

Some agencies are very fortunate to have two officers assigned to a patrol car. With regards to setting perimeter containments this is a great advantage providing that the officers work as a team and have a plan. Preplanning by these two officer teams is the key to success. Discussing numerous scenarios and how they will be handled is a must. "Chase or contain" should be a common topic inside that patrol car. Both officers must have confidence in the other that certain things will be done during a chase and or containment.

Staying together during a foot pursuit is an important tactic. This not only is an officer safety issue, but it will also be a great asset if and when officers decide to contain the suspect. The benefits of having two officers present when a suspect decides to stop and confront is obvious. The benefits of two officers to contain a suspect are not as clear-cut and must be discussed.

Author's note: The two-officer containment tactic about to be discussed at times may require that officers split up to cover two corners of a block. This is done to contain, not capture the suspect. I believe that this can be done safely in most cases as long as officers have clear line of sight of each other, are within a reasonable distance, and have radio communication. The risk of splitting up can be managed. Some law enforcement agencies restrict or prohibit officers from splitting up. Officers must follow the policies and procedures of their agency during any tactical situation.

There are two scenarios that are the most common for a two-officer unit to encounter. The first is a situation where the two officers make the decision to contain prior to the suspect ever fleeing on foot. The vehicle pursuit for example would offer the opportunity for officers to discuss the tactics to be used if the suspect bails out of the vehicle and runs. The officers have time to evaluate the situation and make a choice of chase or contain. Now the officers can communicate their choice to fellow officers.

If the choice is made to set a perimeter containment, the officers must take decisive action when the suspect bails out of the vehicle and runs. As soon as the suspect begins running the passenger officer should quickly exit the patrol car and take a position at the nearest corner of the block to be contained (see Figure 6). The driver then quickly drives to the nearest corner on the short side of the block in the direction that the suspect ran (see Figure 7). If for some reason the driver is delayed and believes that the suspect could have run through the primary block before they reached the corner a second block should be considered.

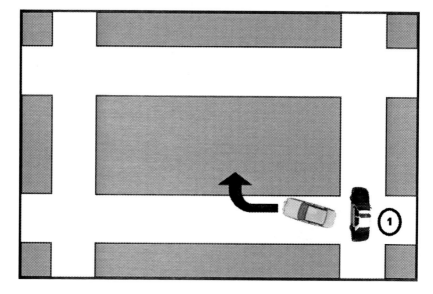

Figure 6. Two-officer containment. As the suspect begins running into the block, the passenger officer exits the patrol car and takes a position behind cover at the corner.

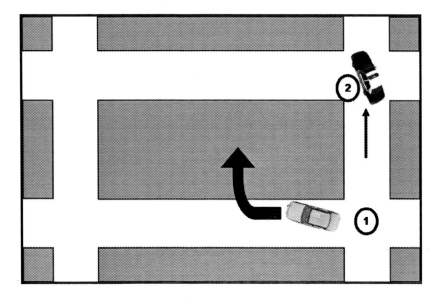

Figure 7. Two-officer containment. The driver officer quickly moves to nearest corner on the short side of the block in the direction that the suspect ran. Three sides of the block are covered very quickly using this tactic.

Now the two officers are in a position to cover three sides of the block to be contained. This can be done very quickly in most cases and has been proven very effective. The officers must continue to communicate to each other about the suspects actions and also give guidance to responding units. All of this must be done while keeping a clear line of sight between each other.

At this point officers can give specific directions to responding units on where they are needed to complete the containment. I like to call this visual distance "reasonable line of sight." Each situation will affect that distance. Two experienced officers that have worked together quite a bit will most likely be safe and comfortable holding the two corners on the short side of the block. On the other hand, an experienced officer training a brand new officer may not want to split-up even a short distance depending on the type of suspect. Each individual officer must determine what is a reasonable line of sight based on the experience of the partner they are working with, the distance between the officers, and the type of suspect they are pursuing. Even the most experienced partners may choose not to split-up when chasing an armed suspect that has fired shots. It is vital for officer safety to maintain a clear line of sight and communication at all times during the setting of the perimeter containment. Officer safety is the priority over any suspect being chased.

The second common scenario occurs when two officers are in foot pursuit of a suspect and at some point during the chase the officers decide to stop chasing and set a containment. This can be less effective than a preplanned containment depending on the position of the officers when the decision to contain is made. If they are close to the corners the technique is the same as was just discussed with the difference being that one of the officers must run instead of drive to the short side corner.

The challenge is when the officer's position is mid-block when the decision to contain is made. Now the officers must run back to the corners in order to cover the block. This takes time and the suspect is most likely still running from the officers. This makes containment difficult if not impossible. Time is not on your side in this case and a second block should definitely be considered for the containment (see Figure 8).

Based on these two basic scenarios, you can see how important training and preplanning are when it comes to successful perimeter containments.

RURAL AREA CONCERNS

No matter what type of area you are patrolling when the decision has been made to contain, the same rules and guidelines apply. Urban areas and residential neighborhoods made it a bit easier when setting a perimeter containment.

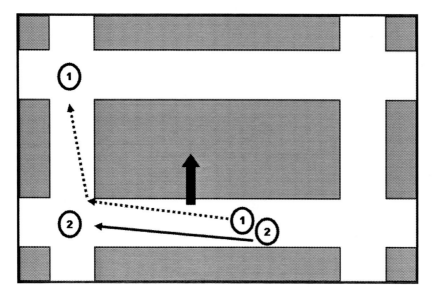

Figure 8. Two officers in foot pursuit. After the suspect turns into the block and the officers make a decision to contain the officers must move quickly to the two nearest corners. This again will cover three sides of the block.

Streets provide clear boundaries and are easy to describe to responding units, but a golf course, rural neighborhood, or wooded area can be contained as well.

It will require the primary officer to be much more descriptive with exactly where they are and where the suspect is running. The boundaries may be a tree line, dirt road, creek bed, highway, or any other natural or manmade landmark that stands out and can be described. Responding units must listen carefully to what is being described by the primary and use good judgment on where to respond. These types of perimeters can be very challenging, but they can be done.

Chapter 3

RESPONDING UNITS

The primary officer during a containment certainly starts the wheels in motion, but the officers responding to the scene are responsible for the completion of the perimeter. The keys to success for responding officers are listening to communications, prompt response, and strategic positioning.

Listening seems simple enough, but as all officers know, air time is limited during vehicle and foot pursuits. The officer in pursuit has the priority for obvious reasons. The information put out by the primary unit determines what actions are required by the responding units. If responding officers are not listening carefully they can easily miss information like the location or description and then take up precious air time asking the unit to repeat the information. Listening and understanding the information is required before an officer can act.

A safe but prompt response by an officer requesting assistance is vital for success. All officers do their best to respond quickly when a fellow officer needs them. When it comes to perimeter containment a quick response to the area increases the chances of successfully containing the suspect. That being said, numerous officers are killed in traffic collisions every year. Officers must not "over drive" when responding to any request. Driving safely is a big part of officer safety.

While responding, officers must pay close attention to updated information from the officer in foot pursuit. Locations and directions of travel oftentimes change quickly and frequently. Attention to detail is very important because it can make the difference in the containment size and exact location. What location the responding units respond to, makes or breaks the containment effort. The first unit to arrive must respond to the corner of the containment area diagonal to the officer requesting the containment (see Figure 9). This allows two officers to cover all four sides of the block. It requires both officers to be extremely alert and to scan both sides of their responsibility until additional units arrive.

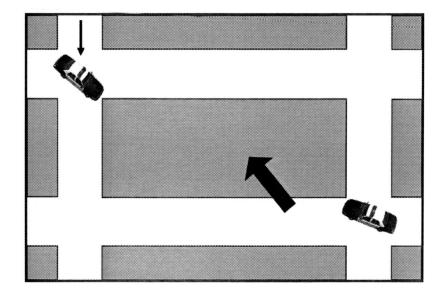

Figure 9. The first officer to arrive to the scene must take a position diagonal to the primary officer. All four sides of the block are now covered (refer to Figure 1).

The next two units to arrive need to take positions at the unattended corners. With all four corners of the containment covered officers will have a good chance of observing a suspect who pops out of the perimeter. If enough assets are available, it is highly recommended that additional units respond to mid-block locations on the long side of the block. This not only takes some pressure off the officers having to watch a long block, but it creates an excellent deterrent to a suspect trying to exit the containment (see Figure 10).

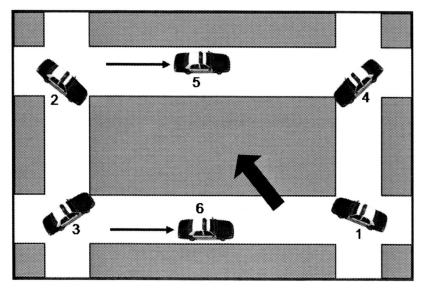

Figure 10. The third and fourth officers to arrive must take positions at the two unattended corners. If additional officers are available mid-block positions are always recommended.

Responding officers should also consider where to go in relation to the size of the containment area. Using the same criteria discussed earlier, responding officers can judge how big of a containment is needed. All an officer really needs to know is the location of the primary officer, the direction of travel by the suspect, and the type of crime in order to put themselves in the best position to cut off the path of a suspect.

As soon as officers arrive at a scene they should exit their patrol cars and find a position of cover away from the police vehicle where they are still able to observe their area of responsibility. Being outside of the vehicle allows officers to see and hear a great deal more than if they were inside their patrol car. Listening for suspects moving about can pinpoint a suspect's location within the containment area. Trash cans tipping, chain link fences rattling, and dogs barking have assisted many officers in narrowing a search for a suspect hiding inside a perimeter.

HOURS OF DARKNESS

In many ways darkness gives a tactical advantage to the suspect who is fleeing. The suspect is able to move much more easily without being seen by officers or residents. Officers can use illumination in a tactical way to take away some of that edge from the suspect.

The use of emergency lighting ("light bars") and sirens as officers approach and arrive at scene is very valuable. The lights are extremely visible at great distances and act as a deterrent to a suspect thinking about crossing a street. Let the suspect know your coming. Even the reflection of the flashing red and blue lights off building walls has made a difference in keeping some suspects from bolting out of a containment.

Spotlights and flashlights can also be used effectively by scanning a large area within the containment to keep a suspects head down. This is particularly important before the containment is covered on all four sides. Anything that keeps a suspect guessing as to what officers can see is a good thing for the officer.

After the containment perimeter is complete and all sides of the area are covered, turning the emergency lights and the patrol car headlights off is in many cases a good idea. Looking for a suspect darting across a dark street is challenging. If you are now looking into a pair of headlights it can actually hinder your view of the block. Officers should experiment during training with these ideas and see what works best for them.

Chapter 4

PERIMETER MANAGEMENT

The most intense and challenging part of the perimeter containment is now complete, but the work is far from over. The perimeter must now be managed and maintained so that a systematic search of the area can be completed efficiently and safely. Setting up a command post is an excellent way to manage assets at a perimeter.

COMMAND POST LOCATION

Where to place a command post (C.P.) is often taken for granted and becomes one of the most common errors at containments. Whether your command post is a supervisor's vehicle with a few extra officers or a SWAT truck, K-9 units, command staff, and a dozen patrol cars, the location where it is located is critical. The risk to officers at a command post is not determined by the size and scope of the operation. It is determined by the suspect's location which in most cases is unknown. The command post should be close to the containment area but certainly not within the kill zone.

All too often the command post is in the middle of the street adjacent to where the suspect was last seen. On numerous occasions officers have learned a bitter lesson about command post locations as suspects are taken into custody from bushes literally feet from the C.P. Remember that the suspect's location could be anywhere within the containment area and officers must use common sense and caution when picking the location of a C.P.

COMMAND POST EQUIPMENT

There is certainly no extra police equipment *required* to have a command post operate, but some additional items should be considered for efficiency.

A dry erase board with markers is one simple tool that can assist officers in keeping a containment organized. This board can be easily stored inside the trunk of a patrol car. Many agencies place a board in each field supervisor's vehicle. The dry erase board can be used to list assets at scene, facts of the case, keep track of any notifications made, and probably most importantly a diagram of the containment.

The diagram should be simple but complete. It should show the shape and size of the area contained listing all street names and any significant landmarks. The locations of the officers holding the perimeter should also be on the diagram. This visual will allow officers and supervisors to know what they may need and where they need it at a glance. On a simple containment this may seem like overkill, but it is good practice for the large scale critical containment that requires organization.

SWAT teams nationwide have used this simple idea for many years. It helps keep things organized so that limited resources are being used in the most tactically efficient way possible. It becomes an excellent tool to brief teams before they leave the C.P. to search. This tool is also helpful when some sort of event such as shots fired or a suspect running occurs during the containment. Officers can more easily respond from the C.P. or be moved to a new location to assist.

After a systematic search has begun the diagram can be used to indicate the areas within the containment that have

been searched. This is obviously important so that nothing is missed and no area is searched more than once by separate officers. As officers or K-9 teams complete a search they can communicate that information to the C.P. and that area can be crossed off indicating what team completed it. This also allows the C.P. to know where every search team is during the search. It becomes important when a team reports a suspect moving inside the containment. The C.P. will have a visual picture of exactly where the suspect is and decide on the proper response.

After the perimeter containment is complete the board can be used to help debrief the incident. The diagram will help officers to see what could have been done differently to help make the next containment even better.

COMMUNICATION

The command post should set the tone for radio discipline during a containment. This can be done in a few different ways.

The first is to set a good example by not using air time when it is not completely necessary. After the containment is set many things can still occur that require officers to communicate their observations. If they cannot get the air time to advise everyone that the suspect just ran out of the perimeter because someone was making an unnecessary broadcast, the suspect may get away and all of the work up to that point is lost. This can be a fine line to walk, but officers should be trained ahead of time as to what is and isn't important to broadcast at a containment.

A second thing that a C.P. can do is to have the primary officer make an informational broadcast after the perimeter is set so that every officer has the vital information necessary to do their job. The suspect description, location and direction last seen, the crime, any weapons seen, and the location of the C.P. are all things that officers need to know. The broadcast should be clear and concise and might look something like this.

"All units on the perimeter. Suspect is a male white, 5-10, 180 lbs., short dark hair, wearing a white tee shirt, blue jeans, and brown boots. Suspect last seen running westbound in the alley north of Oak Street and west of Main Street. Suspect is wanted for robbery and had a blue steel handgun in his waistband. C.P. is in the parking lot on the southeast corner of Main and Oak."

By making a quick detailed broadcast like this, officers on containment will have the vital information they need to complete the mission. It will also help negate many questions over the air regarding the information provided. Remember that all perimeter containments are a team effort and every officer needs the information that the primary officer has to give the containment any chance for success.

The third item is a helpful reminder by the C.P. to all the officers at the scene about radio discipline. Adrenaline can help and hinder any officers' performance during a critical incident. One of the hindrances is that many "pumped-up" officers talk too much on the radio. A simple reminder can control this occurrence in many cases. All officers know what is best to do but may have to be reminded when things are fluid and intense.

This reminder is very important right before any type of search for the suspect begins. During the search is when things can explode quickly and radio discipline is a must. I have seen this scenario many times and it can certainly become an officer safety issue. Officers should also be reminded on containment procedures and holding their positions. This broadcast could look like this.

> *"All units on the perimeter, a search is about to begin. Keep radio communication to a minimum. Search team and emergency traffic only. If the suspect begins running or you hear shots being fired inside the containment, hold your positions unless directed to move. Remember to control ingress and egress at all corners."*

Perimeter containments can be very intense and we are all human. These reminders can make the difference between success and failure and can affect the safety of officers.

RESPONSIBILITIES OF CONTAINMENT OFFICERS

The job of standing at a corner covering a street of the containment can become very dull. It is *the* most important position there is to ensure perimeter success. There is actually a great deal that can and must be done by those officers. Officers on the corners of the containment area have three significant purposes. The first is to observe, the second to contain the suspect by deterrence, and the third is to control ingress and egress.

In order to safely observe, the officer must be in a position with clear line of sight to the next officer on the containment. This observation position should be outside of the patrol car and behind cover or concealment. The suspect is expecting officers to be sitting in their warm, dry police car and that is where the suspects focus will be. By being away from the vehicle the officer is in a position of advantage without being seen and for officer safety. If an armed suspect bolts out of a containment shooting or takes a shot at an officer from inside the containment, those shots will most likely be directed towards the patrol car.

Officers must be extremely alert and suspicious to all activity in and around the perimeter containment area. Many suspects are not content to sit and hide waiting for officers to take them into custody. They will try to exit the perimeter in numerous ways that will be discussed at length in later chapters. Officers must understand that the tactics being used by suspects to exit the area are bold, inventive, covert, and many times desperate. An alert officer will observe many of the methods as long as they are being diligent.

The statements of suspects caught inside perimeter containments are evidence of the value of effective deterrence. Many have told officers that the *only* reason they did not cross a street and get away is that they saw an officer or an officer's vehicle close to their location. In some cases they have stated that they didn't see the officer in the patrol car and would not pop out because the officer's whereabouts were unknown to them. Many suspects have been located hiding in bushes or a trash can within feet of a police vehicle on the perimeter. That speaks volumes to deterrence and the necessity of being alert while holding a corner.

The police vehicle should be parked in the best position to be visible from inside the perimeter and to block traffic from entering the containment area. The emergency lights should initially be illuminated for added deterrence. They then can be turned off if they are interfering with the officer's night vision.

Controlling the ingress and egress of a perimeter is vital. This control serves many purposes from public safety to countering suspects exit tactics. During the containment no citizens should be allowed to drive or walk into the containment area. This is for their safety. A suspect is running loose in their neighborhood and could certainly be a threat to any citizen walking down a sidewalk or entering their residence. Law enforcement never hands a hostage to a suspect and that should include perimeters. Most citizens will understand the slight inconvenience when the situation is explained to them clearly and professionally.

There are exceptions to every rule and if an officer comes across a citizen with an urgent reason to get to their residence inside the perimeter the officer should advise the C.P. and the citizen should be escorted by officers to the residence. Officers should check the residence for any forced entry before leaving a citizen on their own. In only the most exigent circumstances should this be done. Many suspects attempt to gain entry into houses inside of containment areas. Each police agency should discuss this topic before it happens to determine what is a critical reason to allow ingress into a containment.

In a containment for a violent armed felon I cannot think of a reason to allow a citizen into the area short of life-or-death medication needs. This may sound extreme but the risk is high for citizens inside containments because suspects are trapped and desperate. Would you allow your own friends and family to enter the area with a violent suspect on the loose?

Controlling egress is slightly different. Citizens leaving the containment area on foot or in vehicles is certainly permissible but not without some scrutiny. Officers must check inside every vehicle, including the trunk. Some suspects will attempt to exit the containment area by hiding inside of vehicles. Officers should be suspicious and ask a few extra questions of individuals who match the physical description of the suspect. Have the primary officer take a look at people who look close and let them determined if it is the suspect. Do not make a determination on clothing alone. As you will see later, suspects fleeing change clothing for this very reason.

Another tactic that officers can use is to ask citizens that are leaving if they saw or heard the suspect. You will be surprised how much information can be learned about the suspect's current whereabouts from a couple basic questions of people leaving or working in the area. The search can many times be narrowed with the information you learn.

The officer on the corner is the eyes and ears of the containment. This job must be taken seriously and each officer should know the responsibilities it brings. Many suspects have been captured very quickly because of observations or information that a perimeter unit has seen or received.

Chapter 5

WORKING WITH AIRBORNE ASSETS

If you are a patrol officer fortunate to have some sort of airborne assets available to your agency or you are a law enforcement air crew member, then this chapter will give ground and air officers some ideas on how to best handle perimeter containments. Having an air crew over any containment is an incredible tool, however, there are limitations to this tool that all ground officers must understand.

GROUND OFFICERS

In order to use any law enforcement tool efficiently and effectively all officers must have an understanding of the tool and what it needs to work. It is true of SWAT, K-9, detectives, surveillance units, and certainly airborne law enforcement.

In the case of airborne law enforcement involved in suspects running from ground officers, the units on the ground should understand what the air crew overhead can and cannot do, and what information they require to do their job. This understanding is a two-way street. Air crews must have current patrol knowledge to do their job well. When ground and air units work together, a fleeing suspect will be very hard-pressed to escape capture.

Patrol officers need to think ahead whenever possible and request an air unit to respond to their location when the high potential of vehicle or foot pursuit exists. This gives the air crew a chance to arrive before the officers are actually in pursuit. Having an experienced air crew over the suspect as they *begin* to flee dramatically increases the chances for capture. The reality is that this is not always possible for many reasons including deployment of air units, long ETA's, or unexpected suspect actions. But it should be attempted whenever possible.

LOCATION, LOCATION, LOCATION

This topic cannot be stressed enough to patrol officers when working with air units. All police officers have been trained to "always know where you are." This is imperative in order to effectively direct ground and air units to your location when you need help.

Officers must be specific on the location that they need units and communicate it clearly. When an air unit is responding it is even more important to have a specific location for them to respond to. This is because of the crew's large field of view from five hundred feet above the ground.

An example could be this scenario. An officer goes in foot pursuit from a gas station on the northeast corner of the intersection of Main Street and Oak Street. The suspect runs in a northeast direction from that location. The officer makes the following broadcast.

"Unit one, I'm in foot pursuit Main and Oak."

That broadcast will get units to that intersection, but unless they get further information all four quadrants of the intersection will have to be checked to find the officer. This is particularly true for an air crew who can observe all quadrants but can only focus on a small area at a time. A better broadcast would be similar to this.

"Unit one, I'm in foot pursuit Main and Oak northeast corner. Suspect is running northeast from the gas station."

By adding ten quick words the officer has painted a very clear picture of exactly where they are and what direction they need units. The air unit will be able to be effective on the first orbit focusing all of their attention northeast of the intersection. When it comes to specifics on locations air crews appreciate all the specifics officers can give.

SUSPECT LOST PRIOR TO AIR UNIT ARRIVAL

This is the most common situation that occurs even when the agency has excellent air support response time. The officer loses sight of the suspect prior to the air unit arriving overhead. The ground officers should provide the air crew with some vital information prior to the crews arrival so that the air crew can be effective on the very first orbit.

As has just been addressed, the specific location is the most important information that can be provided to the air unit. But that is only the first piece of information required. As soon as the officer has lost sight of the suspect the officer should request a perimeter containment and give the last known direction of travel of the suspect. This should be followed by a basic suspect description and the nature of the crime. This information will paint a picture to the air crew of where they need to respond, where to look for the suspect, and what tactical considerations need to be made. Remember that the air crew is no different than any other responding unit except that they will most likely be more involved in the placement of units to contain the suspect. They need the basic information in order to be effective.

One of the most common errors made by grounds units when using air support is that they fail to communicate information in a timely manner or do not communicate at all.

Flying orbits without knowing what is happening below is a waste of an excellent resource and can easily be avoided. The air crew depends on ground units to provide the information and then they are able to provide the ground units with the support that is most helpful for these situations.

In many cases air crews that have all the basic information have observed the suspect during the first orbit and are able to direct ground units to that individual.

AIR CREW OVERHEAD

As the air unit arrives overhead the primary ground officer must make positive contact with that air crew. Positive contact should be both verbal and visual. The officer should immediately advise the air unit of their specific location and then either wave their arm during daylight or flash their flashlight during darkness to confirm their location.

> *"Air unit this is Unit One. I am on Oak Street five houses east of Main on the north side of the street. I'm waving my arm." Or at night " I'm giving you a light."*

The air crew now knows exactly who they are speaking to and should advise the officer they can see them and to go ahead with the information. The primary unit can now advise the air crew where the suspect was last observed and even point to the specific area. The broadcast should also include the suspects last known direction of travel, and how much time has passed since the officer last observed the suspect. Be as accurate as possible with the time. This is important because it will help the air crew judge how large an area to search and contain.

Sometimes ground officers snicker at the idea of "waving" and "pointing" for the air crew. This is a very effective technique to determine who the air crew is getting the information from and it certainly confirms positive contact. To be most effective the air crew must know where to start and the best way to get that point is from the primary officer directing the crew.

Many air crews have asked the question "primary unit, what's your location?" only to hear the reply "I'm right here under you." Now the air crews are the ones snickering because that reply does nothing for them to find the officer and learn more facts especially when there are numerous officers at the scene. This causes delay, and remember, that the suspect is possibly still on the move.

Remember, providing a specific location, making positive contact, and reporting accurate concise information is a great start to using the air crew to achieve the goal of containing and capturing a suspect. Responding units should follow the guidance of the air crew on exactly where to go. The crew has a bird's-eye view of the entire area and can sometimes determine possible routes of travel based on their training, experience, and physical evidence.

AIR CREW'S ROLE IN PERIMETER CONTAINMENT

Airborne law enforcement is an excellent resource for positive conclusions to numerous scenarios on the ground. When it comes to supporting the patrol officers on the ground, air crews should be playing a major role in both vehicle and foot pursuits situations. In many of these situations an active role by the air crew dramatically enhances public safety, officer safety, and the possibility of capturing dangerous criminals.

Through experience and training air crews are exposed to suspects fleeing on a regular basis. Even with all of that experience, perimeter containment techniques need to be trained, discussed, practiced, and debriefed often so that air crews are prepared for the critical incidents that all law enforcement agencies inevitably face.

OBTAIN CRITICAL INFORMATION

Prior to arriving on the scene of any critical incident the air crew must make every effort to obtain as much information as possible. This may be done just by listening carefully to the broadcasts of the units involved, but many times, it requires direct inquiry by the crew.

After hearing the broadcast of a unit that needs or requests an air unit, the crew should immediately advise they are responding and provide an estimated time of arrival. This informs all officers on the ground of your intentions and the ETA allows them to make solid tactical decisions.

Now is the time to listen carefully to what the officers on the scene are saying. Many times the information you need will be heard on the radio broadcasts. If the information is there the air crew shouldn't have to say a word until they arrive overhead. That is in a perfect world and it doesn't happen all that often, but the point is to listen to get the information so that air time is not taken up with unnecessary questions.

If the information on specific location, description, direction of travel is not being broadcasted the air crew must inquire with specific questions. These questions should be directed to the primary unit and should be clear and concise regarding only the vital information the crew needs at the time. This will allow the crew to be effective upon arrival to the scene.

Critical Information

- *Specific location*
- *Suspects' direction of travel*
- *Basic suspect description*
- *Nature of the crime*

UPON ARRIVAL OVER THE SCENE

The priority on all of these situations is officer safety; therefore, the air crews' first duty should be to verify that all officers that were chasing the suspect are accounted for. This is critical for the safety of the officers in foot pursuit. Many officers have dropped a hand-held radio during a foot pursuit and made a choice to continue to chase. Although this is not a good choice it can and does happen. Some of these officers find themselves confronting the suspect in a rear yard without the ability to communicate where they are and what is happening.

The air crew will be able to assist in these circumstances by searching for a missing officer that is not accounted for. Once that officer is located the crew can direct responding officers to assist. A simple question upon arrival will cover this in most cases. "Are all officers accounted for?" If the answer is yes the crew can concentrate on containing and capturing the suspect. If the answer is no or there is no response at all the crew must now search for the missing officer.

Using the same information used to search for a suspect will assist the crew a great deal. Where was the officer last seen or heard from? What was the direction of travel? How long ago was the officer seen or heard? The answers to these questions should be enough to locate an unaccounted-for officer in most cases. The air crew may have the answers to these questions just from the information they heard while responding to the scene. But if they don't, they must ask for it.

Once all officers are accounted for the crew should be visually searching the area for a suspect still moving. Based on the information received, the crew should estimate the size of the involved area. If the suspect is observed, the crew should broadcast a specific "play-by-play" of the suspect's actions. If the suspect is running within a residential block, the air crew should immediately attempt to contain the block by placing officers at the corners of the block. The first officers should be sent ahead of the suspect to cut off the route of travel.

It is extremely temping for crews to send officers into a back yard after a suspect who is still moving. As good as it looks from the air; it is not always as smooth as that on the ground. Obstacles like fences, gates, and dogs are factors to be considered. By the time the officer reaches the back yard, the suspect may already be into the next yard.

The air crew should contain the block that the suspect is moving inside of and then worry about sending officers into the block to take the suspect into custody. When the block is contained time is on the side of the officers and there is no rush to go in and capture the suspect. Now a team of officers can be directed to the suspects' location. This is safer for all involved and if the suspect leaves the view of the air crew the block is already contained and you know you have the suspect inside.

During an orbit a crew can easily lose sight of a suspect due to obstacles like trees, buildings, and vehicles. In many cases it is only a brief period and the crew reacquires the suspect. Crews must consider that a suspect can move even during a short period of time and might not be where you think he or she is. Containing the entire block eliminates that problem. With the block contained the crew can direct officers to the location where they last observed the suspect. If the suspect is not there officers have the rest of the block to fall back on.

This is a very important concept when it comes to perimeter containment. Unless you are 100 percent sure (a rare thing when chasing suspects) you know the suspect's specific location, contain the entire block and not just one yard or one residence. After the containment is set, officers can concentrate on where you think the suspect is hiding. If you are correct, great, if you are not correct you know the suspect is inside your containment and will be located eventually. Many times it is very close to where you thought the suspect was.

Suspects have learned about airborne law enforcement tactics and know how to move during an orbit. This is a known fact and air crews must consider this when making tactical decisions.

Remember the rule discussed earlier regarding size of containment in Chapter Two.

Do not ASSUME that a suspect is in a particular location without SOLID FACTS to back it up.

If you break this rule *you will lose suspects,* guaranteed. This will become clearer as we discuss the tactics being used by suspects to avoid apprehension.

SUSPECT'S LOCATION IS UNKNOWN

After verifying that all officers are accounted for and quickly scanning the area for a suspect running, the air crew must immediately assist ground officers in establishing a perimeter containment.

The crew's calm communication skills, tactical ability, and knowledge of suspects' tactics will now be put to the test. The air crew must be decisive in directing units to where they are needed in order of priority. Using the information gained from the primary officer the crew should look first at cutting off the route of travel by the suspect. By placing the first responding officer in that path, preferably at the nearest corner, the suspect may be deterred from running further (see Figure 11). The process is identical to that discussed in Chapter 2 except the crew has a unique view from above.

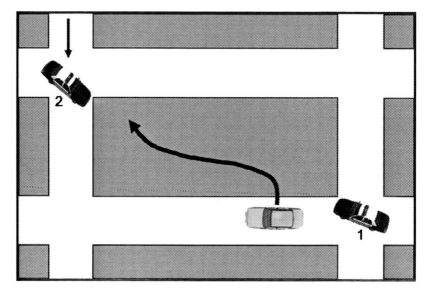

Figure 11. Placing the first officer in a diagonal position to the primary officer is a top priority. This cuts off the path of the suspect and covers all four sides of the block.

All four corners of the containment area must be set for an effective perimeter. If units are available, mid-block positions should always be considered. The crew should direct units in a confident calm manner to where they need to be. This demeanor is more important than it gets credit for. Ground officers' hearts are pumping and adrenaline is flowing on many of these situations. The calming voice over the radio giving directions can change the incident dramatically.

The flip side is when a crew is confused, excited, and barking out orders to these same ground officers. It will make any problem worse and every containment has its problems. A silent crew is no different. Officers are looking for the air crew's help and when they hear nothing they may begin to shut down themselves. These scenarios happen and wanted felons get away.

COMMAND DECISIONS

There are occasions when the ground officers and the air crew have differing ideas on the size of the containment or where officers should be positioned. Understanding that all air units are there to support the ground units it would be easy to say that what the ground units want is what should be done. However, there are factors that *all* officers should consider.

Ground officers should consider the visual advantage that the air crew has over the situation. This view is not perfect, but in many cases it is darn close. Air crews sometimes make observations that ground officers cannot believe are possible. Trust what is being said and listen to the suggestions being made.

Air crews must consider that they rarely have *all of the facts* of the case and should understand the ground officer who may disagree with a tactical decision being made. Air crews should make every attempt to get all the facts so that the suggestions and direction being given is sound.

With all of that said, airborne law enforcement has a responsibility to take charge when an error in judgment has been made or when no decisions are being made. For example, the one block containment or no containment of an area for a suspect who just shot a police officer. That is an error that an air crew can correct with the proper communication skills and tactical insight.

The crew should quickly lay out the facts and then add what needs to be done. In most cases officers will follow the leadership of the crew and correct a critical mistake. This should be done professionally and must be a part of the debrief discussion after the incident to explain the actions.

Containment perimeters are a team effort in every way. The most successful containments have information flowing openly and the capture of a suspect comes before any egos. Mistakes are going to be made and every officer should be willing to step forward and correct the mistake, the capture of a suspect may be at stake.

AFTER THE CONTAINMENT IS SET

The role of the air crew continues to be significant throughout the containment. They should assist in perimeter management any way they can (refer to Chapter 4). The crew has numerous contributions to make for a safe conclusion to any containment including searching for the hiding suspect (with FLIR or binoculars), giving tactical insight to search teams, helping to control ingress and egress, illuminating areas on the ground, and assisting the command post.

Many air crews have FLIR (Forward Looking Infrared) technology on board and should conduct a systematic search of the entire containment area. If done correctly this search will be time-consuming but the positive results are frequent. The best FLIR operators are thorough and patient and they get rewarded for those attributes with "suspect finds."

Giving tactical insight to the search team is a very important function of the air crew. The crew is able to look ahead of the search team and advise them of obstacles, outbuildings, or crossfire with other search teams. Painting a picture of what lies ahead of the search team is vital for officer safety.

Pointing out pedestrians and vehicles approaching perimeter units will assist them in controlling ingress and egress. This is an important part of the success of a perimeter.

At night the tactical use of the night sun can assist ground units in many ways. Illuminating areas of concern and areas ahead of a search team give officers a great advantage over the suspect. Crews should avoid lighting up officers whenever possible, but ground officers must understand that it is going to happen from time to time.

The eyes of the command post are many times the air crew. Painting a clear picture of the containment area is valuable for C.P. personnel to make educated decisions. A good crew should stay very busy during any containment. Communicate and coordinate.

Chapter 6

K-9 SEARCH OPERATIONS

Many agencies have access to K-9 units able to search for suspects. The value of the K-9 search team for perimeter containments is threefold: it saves time, it is effective, and most importantly it lessens the risk to officers.

Different agencies in different regions of the country use canines to search in a variety of ways. Air scenting, tracking, and trailing are all proven canine search techniques. All of these techniques can be applied to perimeter containments.

The key to success for a K-9 search team is to obtain *all* of the information available about the suspect and the perimeter containment itself. The primary officer should provide the team with a detailed briefing of exactly what transpired from the first observation of the suspect to the time the containment was complete. Even the smallest details can make a significant difference in the tactics applied to the search.

WHAT K-9 HANDLERS WANT TO KNOW

- Detailed suspect description.
- Exactly what the suspect is wanted for.
- Is the suspect known to be armed?
- What type of weapon?
- Were there any shots fired by suspect or officers?
- Is the suspect injured?
- Last known location (be specific) of the suspect and direction of travel.

- How fast was containment set?
- Any leads as to where suspect is hiding? (citizen calls, FLIR hits, evidence)
- Does the suspect live in the area?
- Are there any officers inside the containment area?

These are the basics that need to be discussed before any search team begins to search. The more information that a search team has the more effective and efficient the search will be. This information will contribute to officer safety, equipment, techniques, and tactical considerations during a search.

This list will vary depending on the canine search technique used by the agency. Officers should discuss these topics with their K-9 handlers as to what additional information they will require.

PRIMARY OFFICER RESPONSIBILITIES

After the containment is set and the decision has been made to use a K-9 search team to locate the suspect, the primary officer needs to assure that certain rules are followed.

The officer should keep all perimeter units apprised of updated information including the fact that a K-9 team is going to search. This leads to the next responsibility which is to ensure that the area to be searched does not get contaminated for a K-9 search. Any officers who might be inside the containment searching or holding a position should be moved out. The importance of this varies with the K-9 search technique to be used, but it is a good practice to keep officers outside of the perimeter unless absolutely necessary.

The primary officer should speak directly to the K-9 search team as to the facts of the case. Talking face-to-face and not through a third party is best for clarity. Facts tend to get lost or blurred over the radio and through a third party.

The face-to-face also allows search team members to ask questions of the primary officer.

Prior to the search the primary officer should advise all officers on the perimeter that the search is about to commence, where the team is starting, and the direction they will be going. The reminder for officers not to move into the containment discussed in Chapter 4 should be given at this time as well.

K-9 SEARCH TEAM CONSIDERATIONS

Perimeter containments pose a few tactical considerations for K-9 search teams that may not be encountered during other types of searches. Different search patterns, crossfire situations, and excellent communication all play a role during a perimeter search.

Being thorough and systematic during a containment search is very important. The suspect could be hiding anywhere within the containment area and no portion, large or small, should be overlooked or bypassed. An excellent example of this is a search team that completes a search of a residential area except for two yards, one that had a locked gate and the other with a dog in it. Skipping these two yards is a mistake. Every effort must be made to get through the locked gate or to secure the dog. As will be demonstrated in chapters to follow, suspects are very aware that dogs in a yard create problems for search teams and *that* yard is where many suspects will hide. They know that many officers tend to skip over yards with dogs.

Search teams should be creative and persistent when dealing with difficult locations. Contacting citizens to take their dogs inside or to unlock a gate should be a common routine for search teams. Teams that skip yards miss suspects.

For residential blocks there are several search patterns that are helpful for systematic searches. One excellent way to narrow the search quickly in a block that has an alley is to scan the length of the alley. By having the canine team search that area first, it not only clears the alley but it also may give an indication as to which side of the block or even which yard the suspect is hiding in. If no indication is observed then a systematic search of the block can begin.

A second way to narrow a search is to have the K-9 team first check the location where the suspect was last seen. This may give an indication of direction of travel or even locate those few suspects that hide quickly. Again, if no indication is observed the team can pull back and begin the systematic search.

If more than one K-9 search team is available to search the containment there are several types of systematic search patterns to choose from. When two teams are going to search a residential block, an effective pattern is to start at opposite corners on the short side of the block and search into the wind (see Figure 12). The teams should always offset by *at least* one yard to avoid crossfire and interfering with each other. Constant communication is required between the teams to avoid conflicts and to keep that separation.

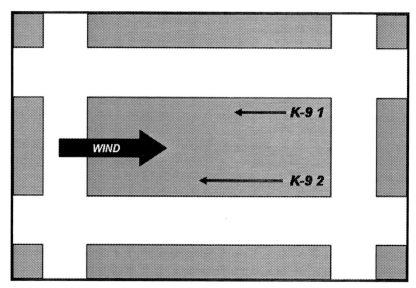

Figure 12. Two K-9 teams conducting a systematic search into the wind is effective and efficient. The teams should always offset by at least one yard to avoid crossfire situations.

For those agencies lucky enough to have four K-9 teams available to search a block, the teams can start at all four corners and work towards each other following the same separation and communication guidelines (see Figure 13). A second four-team pattern for suspects that were lost mid-block is for all four teams to start mid-block and move away from each other towards the corners. This pattern sometimes shortens the length of the search (see Figure 14). Again, it is essential for the teams to stay separated and communicate. In these multiple team searches an air unit overhead is an excellent tool to help with the coordination of the search.

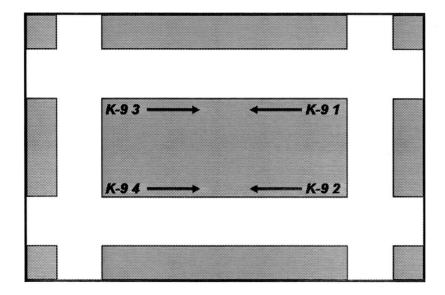

Figure 13: This is an effective systematic search method using four K-9 search teams. It requires additional communication and coordination to avoid crossfire.

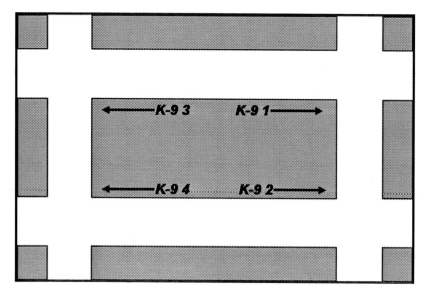

Figure 14: When the suspect was last seen mid-block, this search pattern can sometimes save time and is still systematic.

The teams must communicate information on scent, physical evidence, and witness statements with each other and the command post. The result is that *all* officers involved with the containment are well informed and are ready to respond to changing events.

If a K-9 unit is not available to search the containment and patrol officers or going to search, the same search patterns and systematic search techniques should be applied. A common error is for numerous officers to enter the containment and begin searching on their own. This is not organized or systematic and not only will suspects be missed, it is dangerous for officers. Officers must know who is searching and where they are at all times to avoid crossfire situations.

Being thorough, systematic, and communicating during the search cannot be stressed enough for a safe and successful search of a perimeter containment.

Chapter 7

SUSPECT TRENDS AND TACTICS

When it comes to apprehending fleeing suspects, under-standing the tactics being used by the suspect is as important as understanding the tactics practiced by law enforcement. The trends of the tactics being used by suspects today are significantly different than those of ten or twenty years ago. The criminal element has learned how law enforcement operates and has adjusted their tactics to accomplish their own goal which is to commit crime and *not* be apprehended.

Much of this learning has been done by the criminals themselves through successes and failures from past police contacts. Many suspects running from officers are captured every day; however, a greater number get away. All of these suspects can immediately share their own story with fellow criminals either in a jail setting, if they were caught, or at home with friends if they escaped capture. These stories of success and failure certainly travel quickly through the criminal population and have no geographic boundaries.

This information spreads particularly fast inside prison walls. This setting has always been a school for criminals and the topic of how to escape capture when the police are on your heels is a popular subject.

Law enforcement has actually assisted in this learning curve for criminals through television. Shows like "Cops," "LAPD Life on the Beat," and numerous documentaries on specialized police units have provided some excellent train-ing for the criminal audience. All of these shows were designed to educate and entertain the law-abiding public on what it is really like to be a cop in the United States. That was accomplished based on the ratings and longevity of these types of shows, but someone else is watching as well.

These shows are quite popular among criminals for the exact same reason that the public likes them, entertainment and education. Criminals can educate themselves on how officers conduct certain tactics and then get to hear a detailed debrief of what they just saw. Some tactics are explained very plainly and most criminals can comprehend them.

Officers have been seen explaining modern law enforcement technology such as Forward Looking Infrared (FLIR), less lethal weapons, specialized surveillance equipment, in-car computers, and assorted SWAT items. The taxpaying public certainly has a right to know how all that money is being spent and how well it works to fight crime. These television shows have done a great service for all of us in law enforcement, but every officer must understand that career criminals know more about how police operate than anytime in our history and that fact puts officers at greater risk. It also gives criminals an advantage in escaping capture if they have paid attention in class.

I believe that many criminals have paid attention and are constantly changing how they do things. They are learning from multiple sources and experiences in large cities and small towns. They commit a wide variety of crime and are mentally prepared for what could come next, a patrol car in the rearview mirror. They have tactics in mind to avoid capture and are ready to put those tactics in motion if confronted. Some of those tactics involve violence towards officers if it means getting away. The thought of prison motivates their desperation. They have studied law enforcements tactics and are ready for the final exam.

This is reality across the country and law enforcement must meet the challenge head-on by continuing to modernize equipment and use progressive tactics. Knowledge through training and education is a big part of this challenge. Understanding what suspects are doing when running from officers is the information that is contained in the chapter to follow. This information will be a vital element in the decision making during foot pursuits and perimeter containments.

SUSPECT TRENDS

When it comes to discussing suspect tactics nothing is in stone. Every suspect and every chase is unique, but trends do emerge. None of the suspect tactics about to be discussed are guaranteed to occur when an officer chases his or her next suspect, but they have occurred numerous times in the past by suspects all over America. The trends are what are important for officers to remember so they can prepare for what may lie ahead.

During foot pursuits twenty years ago it was very common for suspects to run a short distance and grab the first good hiding place they saw. Search teams quickly located many of these suspects hiding inside sheds, under houses, and behind bushes. Today this does still occur on occasion, but has become the exception to the rule. More and more suspects are being located a great distance from where they were last observed by officers and many are hiding in close proximity to an officer assisting with a containment.

RUN UNTIL CONFRONTED

This trend clearly indicates that most suspects are no longer content to grab that first hiding spot and wait for K-9 or SWAT to come and get them. They are running as fast and as far as possible until they are *forced* to grab a hiding spot. They are running until confronted by law enforcement.

In this case *confronted* does not necessarily mean an officer with gun drawn standing in front of the suspect, the confrontation is the perception in the mind of the suspect running. It may be the sound of approaching police sirens, or the reflection of emergency lights on a building, or a police helicopter arriving overhead, or a patrol car screeching to a stop at the corner that causes the suspect to now find a place to hide.

Many suspects are using this tactic and the evidence is clear based on where they are being located. More and more suspects are found hiding at the far edge of even large containments many times within feet of a patrol car. Some of these suspects have stated that the only reason they stopped running was the sight of the patrol car at the corner. The officer in that patrol car never observed the suspect but the officer's mere presence deterred a suspect from crossing a street and running out of the containment area.

Finding suspects hiding in the last bush, of the last yard, of the last block of a containment area is a common occurrence. This suspect tactic alone should keep every officer working a perimeter on their toes at all times. The suspect could be hiding in close proximity to their location and may be watching their every move.

PATH OF LEAST RESISTENCE

Studies have been completed in an attempt to place a probability on what direction a suspect who is fleeing the police will turn. This way officers can use these probabilities while searching for a suspect and follow the possible path taken by the suspect and locate them. These studies are interesting and I am sure have some scientific merit, but only in a world without obstacles.

In the real world of fences, walls, gates, dogs, razor wire, trees, brush, vehicles, and any other obstacle you can think of, suspects most often take the path of least resistance. This path has the fewest and easiest obstacles to deal with while running from the police. The suspect being chased does not want to be captured and is going to get as far away from the officer chasing them in the shortest amount of time possible.

Keeping that suspect in mind, let's look at an example. The suspect is running from officers when they run down a driveway into the back yard of an urban residential neighborhood. They observe a five-foot fence with a dog behind it to the right, a seven-foot chain link fence with razor wire straight ahead, and a three-foot fence to their left. Even at a sprint the choice is simple, go left over the easiest obstacle.

Many times the choices are more subtle, but they can be seen and analyzed quickly by officers. The more obstacles the easier it is to predict which way a suspect ran. Air crews have a particularly good vantage point observing paths of least resistance and should always communicate what they see.

Do some suspects still go straight into the razor wire or right over the fence with the dog? The answer is yes. Very few will do that, but it certainly does occur. Most of those suspects have a particular location they are attempting to get to. Remember that understanding this tactic is just one small piece of information that might make a difference in capturing a suspect. All of the facts must be considered with each case.

RUNNING STRAIGHT THROUGH THE BLOCK

This is a very common tactic that goes hand-in-hand with path of least resistance. Suspects have learned that if they move quickly through a block, cross the street, and enter the next block it is very challenging for officers to stay a step ahead. These suspects are correct. Even agencies that are very good at setting quick containments will be challenged by the suspect who does this.

Using an urban setting again with lots of obstacles, a suspect with average speed and agility can run through the width of a block in approximately twenty seconds. That is with a couple of fences. Twenty seconds is not a long time to get an officer to block the path of the suspect. Take away the fences and you can cut five to ten seconds off that time.

This is important for all officers to remember when making tactical decisions on the fly. It is very important for responding units to think of this tactic when deciding exactly where to respond to contain the suspect. Think about how long it took to get to the scene and what kind of obstacles there are inside the block. A decision to contain two blocks instead of one is a good one in many cases especially if the suspect is a serious felon.

DOUBLE BACK

This popular tactic has been documented numerous times and is one that causes problems for officers on a regular basis. Understanding this tactic will make it clear to officers not to assume that a suspect last seen in a certain direction will continue in that direction. Many suspects begin running one way and quickly go the opposite direction after officers have lost sight of them. Choosing to use this tactic is a very conscious decision being made by the suspect and it is one tactic that has been used with success many times.

There are two very common examples of this tactic being used. The first involves any block with an alley. The suspect is being chased by officers down a sidewalk. At some point the suspect turns into the block running between the houses. When the suspect reaches the alley he turns and runs down the alley. The officer observes this turn and assumes that the suspect will continue running down the alley in the same direction he turned. The suspect does continue in that direction but only for a short distance. They enter a rear yard on the opposite side of the block and turn back in the opposite direction moving quickly through yards out of the officers' view. They either continue running out of the block or hide (see Figure 15).

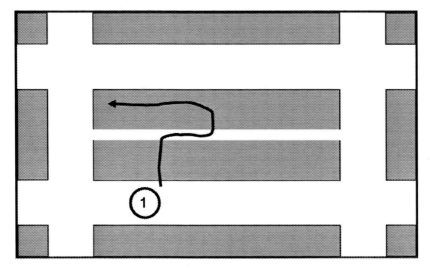

Figure 15. "Double back." Alleys provide several options to suspects and one of those is to double back. Officers should not assume that the suspect is going to continue running in the same direction that they last observed. The double back has become a very common suspect tactic.

Many officers that have had this scenario have stated, "Well, he can't be on this end of the block because he was last seen running the other direction." Officers who understand that double backs are used frequently never make that statement and never assume that a suspects initial direction of travel will remain the same. They contain the entire block and treat all areas of the block with equal respect, and they catch suspects.

The second example is identical in the path taken but without the alley. It has been used to return to a vehicle that the suspect just bailed out of moments before. The key for the suspects appears to be making the turn in a particular direction while still in view of the officers. The officers must show discipline and not be fooled by this action. By containing the entire block and not making any assumptions all the options are covered. Of course, some suspects make that turn and keep running in that direction as far as they can. Containing the block controls that possibility as well (see Figure 16).

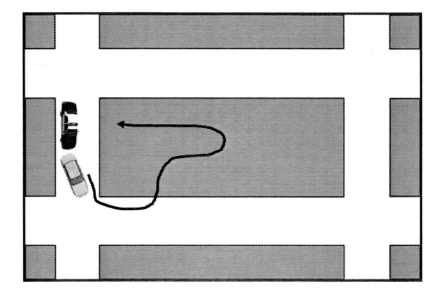

Figure 16. A double back can be used in an attempt for a suspect to return to their vehicle. If an officer holds a corner and contains the entire block the effectiveness of this suspect tactic is limited.

USE OF ALLEYS

In addition to the use of the alley for a double back, the alley itself causes a significant consideration for the officer chasing the suspect. Once a suspect reaches an alley they can run without any obstacles for a considerable distance. The time it takes to get out of that block is cut down dramatically for obvious reasons. Many suspects choose to bail out of vehicles in alleys for that very reason. They are able to put distance between themselves and the officers very quickly.

One tactic that has been used is for the suspect to drive into an alley only a few yards before bailing out and running down the alley. The car that the suspect just bailed out of is now blocking officers from chasing the suspect with the patrol car and they are forced to chase on foot which is to the suspect's advantage in the majority of cases.

Officers need to think a step ahead when they see that the suspect is about to run into a block with an alley and consider their options. A double back could be next or just a fast run covering a lot of ground. Both require quick decisive action by the primary and responding officers.

CROSSING HIGHWAYS

Desperation on the part of the suspect causes actions that are not reasonable at times. Running across any heavily traveled highway has great risk but can be beneficial to a suspect. A suspect running without hesitation across a highway has the same result of a suspect in a vehicle pursuit running through mid-phase red lights without slowing down, it puts distance between them and the officers pursuing. Suspects know that officers will slow down and even stop before crossing the highway or going through the red light, and that creates space and time for the suspect. Once the suspect reaches the far side they have time to move without an officer right on their heels.

This gives an advantage to the suspect even when the officer is prepared for this tactic. If the officer is not prepared and does not respond quickly to this tactic the suspect will probably not be captured. Officers must think a step ahead when they see this possibility in front of them and immediately advise responding units that the suspect may cross a highway and some units should respond to that side of the highway without delay. This foresight will pay dividends when that suspect crosses over and numerous officers are delayed or stopped on the wrong side of the highway.

DRAINAGE PIPES

Many cities and towns have drainage pipes of one type or another. Some of these pipes are large enough to run into without even ducking to avoid hitting your head. I am not sure if this is a rapidly growing trend or a tactic that has been used frequently and we are just catching on, but it is being documented on a regular basis and must be considered by officers who have these pipes within their patrol area.

Suspects are entering these pipes, moving a considerable distance through darkness, and popping up through manhole covers blocks from where they were last seen by officers. If the officer observes the suspect enter the pipe immediate action must be taken by responding units. The primary officer should contain the opening, look at the direction of the pipe, and advise units to contain an area in that direction reminding them to watch the manhole covers for several blocks.

The most common error for this scenario is for all of the responding officers to go to the opening of the pipe. While the officers are standing there formulating a plan to enter the pipe and capture the suspect, the suspect is two blocks away *walking* away from an open manhole cover that they just climbed out. The officers cautiously enter the pipe only to find the opening that the suspect used to escape capture. Clearing the pipe with a search team may be required at some point but containing the surrounding manhole covers and escape routes should be the priority.

What about going right into the pipe after the suspect? This choice should be carefully evaluated by every officer. If the suspect is known to be armed, entering that pipe in most cases has much greater risk than benefit. Being inside a concrete or steel pipe when shots are fired is not where most officers want to be. In addition to that, communication may be inhibited or nonexistent inside of the pipe. A call for help over a hand-held radio when the suspect turns to fight inside the pipe may not make it out to those who need to hear it.

There are two final factors that effect officer safety in this scenario. Most pipes are very slippery and very dark. Even having a flashlight will not help your footing inside of the pipe. All of these things can affect officer safety and should be considered prior to entering any drainage pipe.

Chapter 8

EXITING CONTAINMENT TACTICS

The perimeter containment is set, all four corners are covered and officers are confident that the suspect is inside the containment area. The toughest part of the process is complete, but the suspect is not yet in handcuffs in the back of a patrol car. It is tempting to relax a little at this point but that would be a big mistake. More and more suspects are moving inside containments and attempting to exit the area in a variety of ways. Officers must be aware of these exit tactics and be very alert in order to thwart these attempts.

CHANGE OF APPEARENCE

This is one of the most common of exit tactics and is sometimes even started during the foot pursuit itself. Suspects often wear several layers of clothing and in many cases it is not for warmth. Shedding a layer of clothing can significantly change the appearance of a suspect very quickly. Even while running, suspects have been known to remove a jacket or shirt to alter their look in the hopes that officers will miss the change and ignore them. Why do so many suspects try this? Because so many have had success in the past.

If a primary officer observes a suspect removing clothing during a foot pursuit or a search team locates an item of clothing that matches what the suspect was wearing, they should immediately advise all responding units. This is

75

important information to any officer actively looking for the outstanding suspect. Even without knowing that the suspect has used this tactic all officers should be suspicious of any individual attempting to exit the area even if the clothing description does not match.

There are also many documented cases of suspects stealing clothing from inside the perimeter in order to change their appearance. Some have even shaved or cut their hair in hopes that officers will not stop them as they attempt to walk out of the area.

BLENDING IN

Some suspects have figured out that hiding in a concealed location is not the way to go, it is better to just look like you belong there and officers will ignore you. The list of ways to accomplish this is only limited by ones imagination, but we will discuss a few common blend-in tactics.

During daylight hours many neighborhoods have a great deal of pedestrian traffic inside the containment area. Some suspects have walked out to a sidewalk and started walking with a group of people who they do not know. They continue to calmly walk with the group hoping that an officer at the corner lets the group pass without looking at each individual.

Some of my other favorite "blend-in tactics" are watering the yard, picking weeds, and sitting on a front porch watching all the police activity. Sometimes the suspect is right before your eyes doing something very normal for that area and time of day. Officers must be alert and suspicious to counter these blending-in tactics. If the person watering the lawn matches the general description of the suspect, why not go and talk with them. Sometimes they will take off running as you approach and you have your answer. Some are bolder and will talk with you, but the scrapes on the palms, rapid heart rate, and inability to tell you the address that they are in front of will lead to an arrest.

Most suspects attempting to blend in will first change their appearance in some way.

BOLTING OUT

Occasionally a suspect will just bolt out of the containment area hoping that officers will either not observe the quick run across the street or that officers will not be able to move the containment in time to cut off their escape.

If an officer observes an individual run across the street out of the containment area they should immediately broadcast exactly what they saw. What happens next is very important to maintain perimeter integrity. Let's use a one-block perimeter containment with all four corners covered.

An officer at one of the corners observes an individual run from inside the perimeter across the street mid-block continuing into the houses. The officer broadcasts the observations. The common error is for the four units on the original perimeter to move quickly to the next block where the "suspect" just ran. This is a big mistake. The two units on the side that the suspect crossed should quickly move to the corners of the next block and hold. The other two units should not move at this point creating a new *two*-block containment (see Figure 17).

There is a very good reason not to give up the block that was originally contained: many times the individual that was observed running across the street mid-block *is not the suspect you are looking for*. If you give up what you had and then find out that the guy that ran across the street had a traffic warrant or was chasing his dog, or, well the list goes on and on, you have nothing to fall back on. It has been my experience that approximately sixty percent of the time the person bolting out is not the suspect.

The exception to this is when the officer who observes the individual bolt out can see that it was definitely the suspect

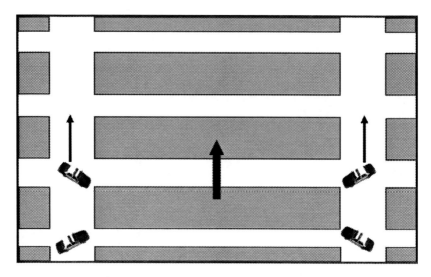

Figure 17. If a possible suspect bolts out of the original perimeter, the two units on that side of the perimeter should move quickly to the next corners and expand the containment to a two block perimeter. Officers should not give up the original area contained.

that you are searching for. During darkness at mid-block it is nearly impossible to identify a running suspect, but if the officer is 100 percent sure that the suspect just ran out, officers should follow the same procedure described above moving the two units to make a two-block perimeter, hold for a minute, and then move the other two units into position for a new one-block containment. This should be done in a controlled manner with clear communication as to who is moving, where they are moving, and when they are moving.

EXITING CONTAINMENT IN A VEHICLE

One way that suspects attempt to exit a containment is inside a vehicle. Suspects have stolen vehicles from within the perimeter, carjacked vehicles, and even hid inside vehicles driven by unknowing citizens who are driving out of the containment area. This simply means that every vehicle that is leaving the containment area must be looked at carefully.

Many times the suspect who has stolen a vehicle from within the containment area attempts to leave the area rapidly driving right past perimeter officers. Those cases will be easy to recognize and handle appropriately. The situations that require more awareness are the suspects who are inside a citizen's vehicle without the citizen knowing. Hiding in the beds of pickup trucks or in the rear seat of vehicles is certainly not unheard of. Citizens attempting to leave the containment area will be numerous depending on the location and time of day and it is not difficult for a suspect to enter a vehicle to go along for the ride.

The desperate suspect who forces a citizen to drive out of the area with them in the trunk or inside the passenger compartment has also occurred. This scenario can cause some tactical challenges when discovered. Perimeter officers must be alert and on guard for this especially if they are searching for a very dangerous individual that is known to be armed.

By controlling ingress and egress of the perimeter, officers can easily combat these exiting tactics. Perimeter officers must stop every vehicle leaving the containment, speak with the driver, take a close look at any passengers, and check every trunk and pickup truck bed for hiding suspects. Although this tactic is not used by a large number of suspects it has been done and none of us know which suspects will attempt this. That being said, if all vehicles are checked at every perimeter, this tactic will never be successful for just a little extra effort by officers.

USE OF CELL PHONES

As the percentage of people who own cell phones has grown dramatically over recent years the number of suspects using this technology to evade apprehension has grown as well. All officers need to note is how many of the suspects that they arrest on a daily basis possess a cell phone at the time of arrest. If that individual with a cell phone had run and was now contained in a perimeter, that phone could be used to exit the perimeter and avoid arrest. There are two well-documented techniques that are used frequently by suspects to exit a containment.

The first is the suspect who is hiding inside the perimeter and calls 9-1-1 to make a false report in an attempt to draw officers away from the corners of the containment allowing the suspect to simply walk away. The suspect may advise the 9-1-1 operator that there is a police officer that needs help at a location not far from the containment area. Another 9-1-1 call that suspects have made is one where they describe themselves in detail and give a location outside of the immediate area where the described person is running.

It is clear what the suspect is hoping officers will do: *leave.* Knowing that this tactic is becoming common, perimeter officers must show discipline and not rush away from their posts which are vital for the integrity of the perimeter. These calls must certainly be checked out but in a controlled manner. If everyone leaves the corners like the suspect is hoping for, then the suspect can easily walk away. The command post or a supervisor should assign a patrol car to investigate the 9-1-1 call while the perimeter is held.

If the communications center has a way of knowing that a 9-1-1 call was made on a cell phone, they should be encouraged to advise officers in the field of that information. This will assist officers in evaluating each call that may be related to the containment.

The second cell phone exit tactic is the more common of the two. The suspect who is inside your containment uses their cell phone to contact a friend to come to the location and pick them up.

This tactic has become common and if the officers on the perimeter are alert and controlling ingress/egress it is easily countered. If no vehicle is allowed into the containment area the suspect can use his phone calling for help till the battery is dead and they will not have success.

Perimeter officers should be alert to vehicles circling the area over and over. This may be an accomplice attempting to assist the suspect. Officers should be alert to suspects bolting out of the perimeter to those vehicles. Prior to that occurring, officers should attempt to stop those vehicles and investigate further. Some of these vehicle stops have resulted in information leading to the suspects hiding location.

CONTROLING EXIT TACTICS

All of these exit tactics are easily controlled by following the simple rule of controlling ingress and egress to the containment area. Having diligent officers checking all pedestrians and vehicles is the key to success. This requires very little effort but has resulted in the capture of numerous suspects.

A bonus to contacting everyone leaving the area is that officers will talk with citizens who observed the suspect running or hiding and are now sharing that information. A simple conversation has led to the suspect's whereabouts on many occasions.

As discussed in Chapter four, the officers that are at the corners may seem to have a dull job but they are vital to the success of the perimeter. More and more suspects are not content to just hide, they are attempting to get out any way they can. These officers must be alert, proactive, and suspicious of anything unusual. The result of this diligence will be more criminals in custody and off the street.

Chapter 9

HIDING LOCATIONS

The topic of where suspects hoping to avoid apprehension hide is extremely broad and everchanging. As long as desperate suspects are running and hiding from law enforcement, the list of locations where suspects choose to hide will never end. Officers across the country are regularly amazed by a location where a suspect has secreted themselves. That is what officers should be thinking about as they are conducting any search for a suspect, the suspect could be anywhere.

Officers who depend on common sense in determining where to search and where not to search are missing suspects. Although common sense is a great asset to possess in most elements of police work, when it comes to looking for hiding suspects it should be temporarily set aside. The reason for this is simple; the suspect you are looking for isn't using common sense in their choice of hiding locations, *desperation* is their guide.

In most cases the most efficient and effective search of a containment is with a K-9 search team. Not all officers have access to K-9 units for every search. You must be prepared to search with a team of officers. That is the perspective taken in the paragraphs to follow.

Taking these facts into account and understanding that there is not a comprehensive "list" of hiding locations, the theme of this chapter will be based on high percentage hiding locations and being thorough with every search.

MOST COMMON HIDING LOCATIONS

On every search, officers must think that the suspect could be anywhere. This will cause officers to be thorough and systematic which will result in suspects being located and officers staying safe.

If we go by percentages alone, there are a few hiding locations that jump out of the pack. Inside, under, and around parked vehicles, trash can and trash bins, and inside or under houses are consistently used by many suspects fleeing law enforcement.

This certainly varies a little from place to place but again there is a simple reason why these three locations are used so often, they are everywhere. Picture a suspect running in your jurisdiction, at some point the suspect makes a decision to hide. What hiding locations are within the immediate vicinity of the suspect when that decision is made? Vehicles, trash cans, and houses are at the top of most officers lists. The result is that many suspects are located by search teams hiding in these locations. Of course there are many other locations where the suspect could be hiding, but we are talking about high percentage locations. Let's look at these top three in more detail.

VEHICLES

Vehicles are everywhere; they are parked in driveways, on the street, inside residential garages, parking lots, and abandoned in back yards and alleys. They are very inviting to a suspect on the run because they can provide good cover and concealment from officers.

Hiding under the vehicle is very common because it is fast and simple. A suspect running at full speed can dive under a vehicle and have instant concealment. They have a barrier above them which is desirable especially if there is a heli-

copter above the scene. They have a view in all four directions from under the vehicle to observe approaching officers.
Suspects have stated that they have watched officers walk
right by them several times without being detected. They
were later located by a police dog that uses its nose and not
its eyes.

Suspects feel pretty secure under there, but they shouldn't.
This is a simple location for officers to locate a suspect. If officers look under *every* vehicle in the search area, these suspects will be easily caught. It does require that officers get
down low to the ground from a position of tactical advantage
and illuminate the entire area under the vehicle. A quick
look can be a mistake as some suspects will secrete themselves up into the undercarriage of some larger vehicles.
They will also tuck themselves tight against one of the wheels
and depending on the officers angle could be missed by a
quick glance. Officers must take that extra few seconds to be
thorough and not miss an easy find.

Hiding under vehicles: If you walk past this vehicle without looking under it, would you observe the suspect? Every vehicle must be checked thoroughly or you *will* miss suspects.

I used the word *illuminate* when describing what officers need to do when checking under vehicles. Carrying a flashlight during daylight hours should be routine for all officers. We can never predict when we will need to illuminate an area or location for officer safety. This is the first of many examples of that while conducting a search. Looking under a vehicle during the day without a flashlight can lead to missing a suspect. Shadows, debris, and a suspect up against any object can fool the eyes even with illumination. Officers should give themselves every advantage possible, carrying a flashlight at all times is one way to do that.

A safe and effective technique for looking under vehicles is to use two officers, one to illuminate the area under the vehicle and the second to search. The officers should be at the same end of the vehicle but on opposite sides. The tires can be used for cover. As the first officer lights up the area, the second can check the area carefully. If there is a suspect under the vehicle they will most likely key on where the light is coming from and not observe the second officer.

Hiding inside of vehicles provides additional cover and concealment for the suspect, but it also requires more effort. Many vehicles are locked which would require the breaking of a window by the suspect. This is unlikely because it takes time, makes unwanted noise, and leaves evidence for officers to detect. If the suspect *does* find an unlocked vehicle, they may use it.

Officers must look inside every vehicle they pass inside the search area. Many suspects will cover themselves with a blanket or jacket once inside for additional concealment and also lock the doors behind them. If something doesn't look right inside a vehicle it should be investigated further. Be suspicious and don't be fooled by a simple suspect tactic.

Inside the bed of pickup trucks is also a common hiding spot. Many pickup truck beds already have items that can be used to cover the suspect for concealment. Officers should search every pickup bed and again must be thorough in their search.

Air crews conducting a FLIR search of an area should always pay particular attention to all vehicles in and around the search area. In most cases of a suspect inside or under a vehicle the heat signature will be subtle. The vehicle must be looked at from all four sides for best results. If there is a question about something you observe always have a ground officer check it out for you. A suspect hiding under a vehicle that is still hot from being driven will be extremely difficult to detect. That is another good reason for ground officers to check every vehicle no matter what the heat signature.

TRASH CANS

Trash cans and trash bins are everywhere as well. Residential trash cans and commercial type trash bins are more prevalent than ever. Many communities now have three different trash cans for each residence to handle trash, recyclables, and grass clippings. Some of these cans are large enough for a suspect to hide inside of and they do quite frequently.

Understanding that trash receptacles are one of the most common hiding locations used by fleeing suspects requires officers to look inside every can. This must be done with officer safety as a priority. One technique that can be used requires at least two officers, one to carefully open the lid while a second illuminates and checks inside the can. The officer opening the lid should quickly step away from the can after the lid is opened. This allows the searching officer to have both hands on their firearm and or flashlight and full concentration on a possible threat that could arise. This technique is for routine checks of trash receptacles, not for ones where officers believe the suspect is inside of it based on a FLIR hit, K-9 alert, or other information.

Air crews must look very carefully at all trash receptacles with the FLIR. Plastic trash cans show heat very well from a suspect hiding inside. Unfortunately, decomposing grass inside a can looks almost identical on the FLIR. Air crews should advise ground officers of the heat signature being detected from a trash can and let the officers carefully check it for a possible suspect. The air crew should not assume that the heat signature is or is not a suspect hiding inside the can. They should advise the search team of what they observe and leave the rest up to the ground officers. By doing this search teams will hopefully treat each of these checks the same and not let their guard down. When air crews say things like "this is probably just decomposing grass in this can, but could you check it" that causes a slight letdown in the searching officer's mind and tactics *could* be affected.

Larger metal trash bins create a tougher problem for FLIR searches. It takes longer for the heat signature to show through the metal depending on where the suspect is hiding inside the bin. The result is that a bin with a suspect inside giving off heat may look exactly like the bin next to it without a suspect inside. On larger bins with two-piece lids a heat signature can sometimes be observed along the crack between the two pieces.

The bottom line for ground officers is to understand the limitations of FLIR technology and discuss it with your air crews. Treat every trash can as if the suspect is hiding inside no matter what you hear from the air crew. Officer safety is the priority and you should always error on the side of caution when searching for suspects.

HOUSES

Inside and under houses has always been a favorite of suspects. Getting inside a residence gives a very distinct advantage to the suspect, but they are not home free. There are several ways that a fleeing suspect can do this.

The first is probably the most common way to enter a house to escape capture and that is to be invited inside by a "friendly." Suspects who are running in their own neighborhood know which doors will open for them if they are on the run. They will make their way to those doors for help and get inside out of the view of all officers. This is a difficult scenario for officers because it rarely leaves physical evidence and can happen very quickly. Officers might have prior knowledge of a certain suspect or a certain "friendly" house in a neighborhood and can work on that information. Otherwise officers can hope for a citizen tip leading them to a certain house or a K-9 alerting on a door to lead them to the suspect.

Forced entry has become more common but many times the forced entry creates a citizen call from inside or next to the location to lead officers to a particular house. This type of entry very often leaves physical evidence that an alert search team will observe during a systematic search. Any indication of forced entry, however slight, should be investigated further.

In these cases officers that door knock a house with strong indications that the suspect forced entry often find themselves speaking with a frightened resident who is scared to say what is *really* going on. Officers must be cautious, thorough, and suspicious when they have evidence to believe that a suspect is inside despite the scared residents' statements that everything is fine.

If and when officers enter a house to search for a suspect, the search must be systematic and thorough. There are numerous places to hide inside a residence; however one place that must always be considered is the attic. This is a very common hiding place and must never be overlooked. Physical evidence that a suspect entered an attic is often present around the opening to the attic.

BRIBERY

Occasionally a suspect may try and bribe their way into a residence. Although this is rare it does occur and normally involves bank robbery suspects. Not tough to figure out why, cash in hand.

The vast majority of these types of cases result in a citizen calling 9-1-1 and advising officers where the suspect was last seen after the failed bribery attempt to get inside. This quickly narrows the search and the suspect is taken into custody a short time later.

UNDER HOUSES

In certain regions of the country many older houses sit on a raised foundation where there is no basement. This creates a crawlspace anywhere from one to four feet with a dirt floor. In most cases there are numerous screened air vents leading to this space. If these types of houses exist in your jurisdiction you must pay very close attention to them during the search for a suspect.

Again this type of location is popular because of its frequency and great cover and concealment. Once under the house the suspect can sit undetected in darkness. Many times there is little or no evidence that a suspect entered this crawlspace. Occasionally officers will observe a screen or vent ajar or broken that will lead them to the crawlspace. This is certainly not always the case and every crawlspace inside the search area should be checked carefully. This has been a popular hiding location for decades and is still one of the top percentage locations to locate a suspect hiding.

A K-9 search team is the most efficient and effective way in determining that a suspect is hiding under a house. Even after a K-9 has alerted on scent and it is determined that the source is under the house, this hiding location can cause some unique tactical problems. Narrowing the search using a K-9 under the house is possible, but risky for the dog. Pipes, wires, tight quarters, darkness, and a wanted suspect are all hazards to the dog and officers.

Many of these crawlspaces have additional foundation walls that a suspect can move behind to avoid being seen from a particular angle. This may require an officer to carefully enter the crawlspace if the entire space cannot be visually cleared using all available openings. The tactical use of flashlights will be very helpful in clearing the crawlspace. Of course, if the suspect is known to be armed or believed to be armed the tactics used to clear a crawlspace change dramatically. Officers should use *all* available techniques and resources before entering the crawlspace. Some of these situations may require SWAT personnel to complete the search and apprehension, particularly if the suspect is armed.

Understanding that it may not be practical for SWAT to be requested for every suspect hiding under a house, patrol officers should be prepared to handle these situations as they arise. Agencies must consider this scenario and consider some specialized equipment for patrol officers in the field. All of this equipment is also vital for clearing attics.

High-intensity portable lights, extendable mirrors, and less lethal munitions are three types of equipment that dramatically increase officer safety for subfloor and attic searches.

These items are easily stored in the trunk of a patrol car and can be quickly deployed.

Officers can illuminate the space and use the mirrors to search before physically looking inside. If a suspect *is* located in a tight space, less lethal munitions provide tactical options for officers attempting to take the suspect into custody. Officers must train regularly with this equipment to become proficient.

I am certainly not suggesting that every crawlspace needs to be physically cleared by officers within the perimeter containment. That would not be at all practical in the vast majority of cases. Officers should use all of the facts and evidence to determine which crawlspaces require additional attention. Again this is best accomplished by the use of a K-9.

ADDITIONAL HIDING LOCATIONS

Officers who are responsible for searching a containment area must be in the correct mindset to be effective and efficient. Officers must consider all of the possible places the suspect could be hiding and check them thoroughly. This is, of course, different on every search. For instance, a search in an urban area is going to have a wider variety of locations to hide than a search of a rural or wooded area. However, that search in the wooded area will be more difficult and challenging in numerous ways.

Any type of landscaping, trees, brush, ivy, bushes, and ground cover can be difficult to clear. Many suspects hide using this natural cover which provides excellent concealment. An officer can be within a few feet of a suspect hiding in thick brush and never see them. This creates an officer safety problem that is not easy to solve. Again, using a K-9 for this type of search will enhance officer safety and locate a suspect much more quickly, but that option may not always be available.

Officers should move slowly and check any type of ground cover from as many angles as possible. Many times the suspect can be observed only from a certain angle. This is true of many hiding locations and the officer that shows patience while searching will have the advantage.

Trees provide a variety of options for a suspect. Some suspects hide up in the tree itself while others use a tree as a ladder to reach a rooftop or other location to hide. Many officers get so focused on searching things right in front of them that they forget to look up. Many suspects are located hiding on the rooftops of sheds, garages, and houses adjacent to trees. Some of these same suspects have stated that the reason they hid above ground level is because they have had contact with a police K-9 in the past and did not want to have a second contact.

OUTBUILDINGS

All types of outbuildings including sheds and garages are popular hiding locations for suspects. These locations provide the concealment of a house but because they are not occupied the risk of being observed by a resident is significantly less.

Most outbuildings have numerous items inside that can be moved to conceal the suspect inside the structure. These same structures are not very secure in most cases and are easy to gain access to. These are all appealing qualities to a suspect looking for a location to hide.

Officers should carefully clear all outbuildings during a search. Looking for physical evidence of forced entry should be routine. Any advantage officers have prior to breaching a door enhances officer safety.

STAIRWELLS

Stairwells of all types provide a few options for suspects. Hiding under a stairwell and on the landing at the top of a stairwell are both very common.

Hiding under some types of stairwells provides suspects a small tight space to conceal themselves in darkness. These types of stairwells are very common in most communities and have easy quick access for the suspect on the run.

The landing at the top of a stairwell is an important hiding location to discuss. An officer can easily miss a suspect hiding there if they don't clear it properly. Using the example of a stairwell leading up to a second floor landing, if an officer stands at the bottom of the stairs and visually clears the stairwell they can easily miss a suspect lying prone on the landing. Officers should move slowly up the stairwell until the entire landing is clearly visible. Officers who choose not to do this will miss suspects.

Stairwells must be carefully checked to avoid missing suspects. A quick glance up this stairwell does not reveal anything unusual. Would you keep walking or take the time to check the landing at the top of the stairs?

As you move slowly up the stairs something unusual begins to come into view.

This suspect would have been missed if you did not take the time to properly clear the landing. Being thorough and systematic pays big dividends when searching for suspects.

DOG HOUSES

This is one of my favorite hiding locations to talk about because so many suspects have used this location in the past and have escaped capture. This is based on the statements of suspects who are found inside dog houses. Many are shocked that officers even looked there. More than a few times suspects have stated "I can't believe you got me, cops never look there." This is something that suspects believe and it is why they choose to hide there.

Dog houses with dogs present, some even chained to the dog house, are not immune from suspects hiding inside. Checking inside each of these dog houses will sometimes take additional time in securing a dog, but it will eventually pay off. A few suspects have been found hiding inside the dog house with most of their clothing wrapped around their arm like a thick sleeve to defend themselves from the pit bull outside. *That* is desperation and willingness to take risks to get away.

Air crews conducting a FLIR search should never assume that a heat signature from a dog house can only be a dog inside. They should simply communicate what they observe to ground units and those units should take a closer look. The vast majority of the time it is a dog sleeping inside, but are you willing to gamble on which time it is going to be the suspect you are looking for?

HOT TUBS AND SPAS

Both in-ground and above-ground hot tubs and spas cannot be ignored as potential hiding locations. Many of these spas have covers which provide concealment. Even if there is water inside they need to be checked. Suspects have been located inside spas filled with water and covered. The suspect's heads were barely above the water line in order to breathe. In some of these cases officers had searched the yard with the spa and never opened the cover to look inside. K-9 search teams later searched the same yards and immediately alerted on the spas. The wet suspects were taken into custody.

BETWEEN STRUCTURES AND UNDER LEANING ITEMS

Suspects attempting to hide seem to love tight spaces. The small space between a building and a wall for instance is a very popular hiding location. Sometimes the space looks so small that officers say "he could never fit in there." The suspect is then located in that same tight space and the fire department needs to assist the officers in getting the now trapped suspect out of the hiding spot. Expect the unexpected when searching for desperate individuals, and remember that common sense is not part this equation.

While searching for a suspect officers should pay particular attention to anything leaning against a structure that creates a gap at the base. A very common example is plywood but it can be anything. That small gap provides a space to dive into for a running suspect. Many suspects take advantage of these leaning items for a place to hide. Taking a close look at these tight spaces will pay off with suspects being found.

CONCLUSION

These are just some of the endless possibilities of hiding locations. Every officer has a unique story where they have located a suspect hiding. The suspects found rolled up in carpet, hiding inside a wall, or buried under a pile of trash are not the norm but do provide all of us with an important lesson, the suspect we are looking for could be anywhere.

Searches should be conducted with officer safety as the priority. Officers must be thorough, alert, and observant. They should expect to find the suspect in every trash can they open and under every vehicle they check. This will keep them alert and safe.

Chapter 10

TRAINING TO MEET THE CHALLENGE

A professional sports team would never dream of playing a game without training and practicing for the contest. A team that did this would surely lose and risk injury to its players. A coach that would send their team into battle depending on them to "learn on the fly" would not last very long.

Policing the streets of America is not a game, it becomes a fight for life or death at times and the public is depending on law enforcement to protect them. Unfortunately, many officers have not received any training of how to capture a fleeing suspect other than what they have learned on their own through trial and error. They are ill-prepared for the event that *is* going to take place, and in police work the time and place of that event is not known until it begins.

Putting criminals behind bars and off the street is a large responsibility that has been given to law enforcement. Officers spend countless hours learning about search and seizure, traffic laws, self defense, conflict resolution, and officer safety topics. Some even receive training on foot pursuits. Formal training on what to do if you lose sight of the suspect is very rare, yet this occurs countless times a day to hard-working officers across the country.

If law enforcement agencies are truly committed to apprehending criminals and keeping their officers as safe as possible, they must focus more training into this topic. Officers need training, experience, and practice in order to learn any tactic or technique. In the case of learning about perimeter containment, officers must also have a working knowledge of what criminals are doing to avoid capture.

Perimeter containment is a proven technique that requires consistent training of all officers in the field. If some very basic rules are followed by everyone involved it can be a simple task. But it requires training and practice.

START IN THE CLASSROOM

Most training starts in a classroom setting. This is an excellent forum to provide basic knowledge to personnel on perimeter containment techniques. This will provide a base to work from as the officers' progress.

The information contained in the first six chapters is vital for any agency that is using or plans on using perimeters to capture fleeing suspects. Understanding each of the roles involved in the perimeter and how they are connected is a must. An officer in foot pursuit is counting on the responding officers to do the right thing. Although the roles are very different the goal is the same, capture the suspect.

By breaking down this technique into responsibilities for each role (primary officer, responding officers, supervisor, and specialized units) it allows officers to learn the information in several ways depending how they are involved in the incident. Keeping it simple and emphasizing communication will be beneficial later.

Tabletop exercises are extremely helpful in a classroom setting. Breaking up into small groups and giving each a scenario of what needs to be done to contain a suspect draws out ideas and discussions on the best ways to accomplish that task. Many unique ideas come out of these tabletops and they need to be shared with everyone involved in the training.

ROLL CALL SETTING

This is a great setting to discuss tactics and perimeter containment. It keeps the topic fresh and continues to spark discussion. None of us know when an incident is going to occur that requires us to use the training we have received. This is why the beginning of the work day is an excellent time to remind personnel of different policies and procedures. As officers leave the station and start their shift the information received a few minutes earlier is fresh in their minds and can make a difference when they are suddenly in a critical situation.

All of us have experienced stressful situations where after the incident you realize that what you had just done was the result of past training kicking in. This is very clear in use of force events particularly those that involve deadly force. Many officers will say that they had just qualified on the pistol range or had just discussed shooting policy in roll call prior to the event and that it definitely was a factor in how well they handled a stressful situation. Foot pursuits and perimeter containment fall into this category. They begin quickly and cause mental and physical stress that must be managed. Training is certainly the key to success.

PRACTICAL TRAINING

After a good base of knowledge has been taught in a classroom, it is time to apply the information to some practical training.

One very effective way to test what has been learned and to practice the technique is to find an area where a foot pursuit and perimeter can be staged. Industrial areas after hours work very well for these training scenarios.

Before starting the training, strict guidelines should be made clear and all weapons should be downloaded and inspected for safety. Emphasis should be placed on working at half speed to avoid injury and vehicle collisions. Make it clear what the training is attempting to accomplish. In this case it should not be speed, it should be communication and where officers respond.

An officer should be assigned the role of "the suspect." They should be briefed on exactly what is to be accomplished and given strict parameters on where they can run. The first few times that this training occurs, the "suspect" officer should be told to move only at a walk to avoid capture. The foot pursuit is not being practiced in this scenario; it is the containment being set. Again, speed is not important at this stage.

Even at this slow pace you will see how important responding to the right location is to contain a suspect. The walk will lead to a jog and then a run as officers' progress and learn the technique.

The job of primary unit should be assigned each time and rotated so each officer gets the opportunity to communicate the suspect's actions and request a containment. This officer should also be given guidelines and be reminded that the containment is what is being practiced, not the foot pursuit.

The responding units should be a reasonable distance away from where the suspect is going to run and they should not be staged all together at one point. This will add some realism to the scenario. They should be reminded not to overdrive when responding to the foot pursuit. Make it clear that they will be evaluated on *where* they respond and not how fast they get there. The "suspect" officer will be moving slowly and so should they.

Several officers should be strategically placed to observe the actions of the primary and responding officers. What they observe as well as what the "suspect" officer observes will be vital in a critique of the training. They should pay close attention to what is said and where officers respond based on the communication.

Be prepared to go through this scenario numerous times till things start to go well. It is not as simple as it sounds even at slow speed. This is just a way to instill good communication, good containment response, and the correct mindset for all involved.

Be sure and follow strict safety guidelines during this type of training.

- All weapons should be unloaded and inspected.
- The "suspect" officer should not be touched.
- Do not over drive.
- Choose a training area that is appropriate for the time of day.
- Remind officers to work at slow speed.

After each scenario everyone involved should meet and discuss what went well and what can be improved on. The "suspect" officer will have a good view of the good and the bad and should be honest with officers so they can improve. The suspect role should be rotated from time to time to give everyone a unique perspective on perimeter containment.

The more that this is practiced, the more effective and efficient it becomes. Be patient with the progress and never be in a hurry to speed things up. The time for speed will be in the field with the real suspect running.

REAL EXPERIENCE

The true test is when a criminal chooses to run from law enforcement and the primary officer decides to contain the suspect. Now is the time to put all of the information, training, practice, and experience to work.

Some perimeter containments will be easily set while others will be difficult. The fact that the attempt is being made is more important than it may appear. Each time officers experience a containment they learn from it no matter what the outcome. Even if officers know they may not spend any time searching for a particular suspect, it doesn't hurt to set up a containment just for practice. Breaking down a perimeter containment is quick and easy, "thanks for your response;

we are breaking down the perimeter." The units leave the location and continue on with the shift.

Some officers are very hesitant to call units in to set up a containment because they are not sure what they have. This is, of course, very common in police work and officers should not hesitate to set a perimeter on a suspect who has run from them only because they are not sure if they have a crime.

Examples of this type are very common. An officer observes a male in his early twenties loitering in a parking lot looking into vehicles. When the suspect observes the officer driving into the parking lot he runs out of the lot into a residential neighborhood. The officer pursues, but when the suspect runs between the houses and out of the officers' view the officer stops and returns to the parking lot. Not knowing what they had, the decision was made to stop the chase and let the individual get away.

Now back in the parking lot the officer discovers several vehicles with broken windows and radios missing. The officer is then flagged down by a citizen who reports that a male is his early twenties was seen breaking into a car several minutes ago. The description given matches the suspect who ran from the parking lot and is now somewhere with several radios that do not belong to him. The officer can now fill out a detailed crime report and hope to catch the suspect another day.

Setting a perimeter does not require that much effort. After the units arrive and the containment is set, the officer can return to the parking lot and investigate what if anything criminal has occurred. If the above situation is the case, the officer can now complete a search for the suspect and capture a car burglar. On the other hand, if the officer returns to the lot and finds no evidence of a crime they can advise units to break down the perimeter. It was one more perimeter under everyone's belt for experience. The next containment will be even better and that next perimeter may be the most important one in a career.

I have said many times that all of the perimeter containments for car thieves and burglars and even robbery suspects are just for practice. All of those crimes are serious and we should do our best to capture every one of those suspects, but by gaining experience on those criminals, officers are preparing themselves for the day that a critical incident occurs when it is vital to contain a suspect.

None of us know if and when we will encounter a scream over the radio, "Shots fired! Shots fired! Officer down!" These are chilling words that none of us ever want to hear and yet many of us have heard. Now is the time when the perimeter containment techniques learned must be used decisively and effectively. This situation is going to cause very unique stress on officers and supervisors. Agencies that have not been practicing perimeter containments are not going to be effective in this case when it is happening.

Even departments that use this technique on a nightly basis struggle with it during an officer down. It is very easy to get tunnel vision when one of your own is injured. Everyone is responding to the location where the officer is down and not thinking of where the suspect is running. Training and experience will kick in even under this type of pressure, but only if this situation has been discussed and trained for in the first place. Have a plan, execute the plan.

DEBRIEFS

The debrief may be one of the most underused training tools in existence today. It is an excellent technique that seeks continual improvement in every aspect of any tactical operation. It can be used during training and real-life scenarios and is a required tool of improving on perimeter containments. Nothing goes perfectly, so ask the question, "What could we have done better?"

In order for a debrief to be effective it must be done in a positive way. No matter how good we are we can do better.

Don't seek to find fault, seek to improve. Some basic debrief ground rules must be followed to benefit from the debrief.

The first rule is to "park your ego at the door." We are all human and make mistakes, some minor and some major. Opening up to criticism is difficult for many police officers, but it is part of the learning process. A good way to handle this is to look at what you could have done better before looking at others. A little humility goes a long way in a debrief.

The next rule is that rank has no place at a debrief. Everyone at a debrief should be equal in accepting criticism as well as praise. If a high ranking individual is not open to this idea, the debrief will be significantly less effective. Open communication is the key to a productive debrief and no one should be exempt from trying to improve. A good leader will create an atmosphere where everyone feels safe to share ideas and constructive criticism.

The next two rules go hand-in-hand. All criticism should be constructive and everything said during a debrief should be said in a respectful way. An excellent debrief can fall apart quickly when a single individual is disrespectful when being critical. This is the one place in a debrief where rank should facilitate, and ensure a positive environment is maintained. Having a senior officer or supervisor take a lead role in a debrief is a good practice as long as they are an equal part-ner during the debrief.

Every individual involved with the operation should have the opportunity to speak during the debrief. That means from the highest ranking supervisor to the newest probation-ary officer. Everyone sees things from different perspectives and rank and experience do not always equate to more value in what is said at a debrief.

The debrief does not have to be a long and drawn-out affair for the majority of incidents, but it should be done as often as possible. Most units that debrief often say that they really should do it even more often. It is an art and needs to be practiced. It is a great way to constantly improve at setting perimeter containments. Remember that the time to bring up an issue is during the debrief. Critical analysis of an event in front of your peers takes courage. "Gossips" choose not to speak up during a debrief with a criticism or concern and then talk about the issue later over coffee. This is nonproductive and destructive.

CONCLUSION

I have participated in over 1500 perimeter containments in my law enforcement career. I have yet to see "the perfect perimeter containment." I have seen many perimeters come very close to achieving perfection but there is always something that does not go smoothly. Fortunately, perimeters do not have to be perfect to have success.

Setting a perimeter containment and capturing a suspect is a complex task. There are so many factors that affect every small element of the technique. Things change at high speed and decision making is at its peak for all involved. Adrenaline has a lot to do with why containments are never perfect and that is something that we can only manage through training, experience, and good decision making. The key is to limit the mistakes by following the general rules and guidelines each time you are involved in a perimeter no matter what your role.

In police work experience can be measured not only by the events that each individual officer experiences, but also by the experiences of fellow officers. All of us have found ourselves in a situation that was new to us, but one that you had heard about from a partner, at roll call, from a seminar, or an article. This knowledge was beneficial in handling the situation. That is what I have tried to achieve with what you have just read in this book. Whether you are setting perimeters on a nightly basis or only a few a year, the more information you have about suspect tactics the better decisions you are going to make trying to contain and capture them.

I truly hope that every law enforcement officer who reads this book and applies the knowledge gained will have a positive effect on putting more criminals in jail. The satisfaction of placing the cuffs on a dangerous suspect that you contained and captured with communication, teamwork, perseverance, and sound tactics is difficult to describe to people outside of law enforcement. May you feel that satisfaction often and get home safe at the end of each shift.

INDEX

ABOUT THE AUTHOR

Jack H. Schonely has been working on the front lines of law enforcement in a wide variety of field assignments for over 24 years. Starting as a Deputy Sheriff in Berks County, Pennsylvania and then moving to the mean streets of Los Angeles, California as a member of the Los Angeles Police Department, he has seen firsthand the changes in how the police and the suspects they are chasing are doing business on a daily basis.

After joining the LAPD in 1983, Jack worked as a patrol officer where he was first exposed to the concept of "perimeter containment" as an effective way to apprehend suspects fleeing on foot. The 1980s were a busy time in Los Angeles with gang wars and a crack cocaine epidemic both at their peaks. During most of this time Jack was assigned to 77th Street Division in "South Central" Los Angeles and was involved in perimeters on a nightly basis.

Jack became a field training officer before transferring to an undercover assignment working Hollywood Vice. After completing the 18-month vice tour he was selected as an element member in the department's Metropolitan Division. There, he worked across the entire city working crime suppression, bank stake-outs, VIP security, and crowd-control details. This is where Jack was assigned during the 1992 Los Angeles Riots.

In late 1992, Jack applied for a position as a K-9 handler within the Metropolitan Division. He was transferred into that job and spent the next five years searching for LA's most dangerous criminals. He participated in over 700 high-risk K-9 searches as either the primary dog handler or search team member. More than 300 of those searches resulted in the capture of the suspect. Jack interviewed numerous suspects after their capture to learn how they attempted to avoid being caught.

His next challenge came working as a Tactical Flight Officer (observer) with LAPD's Air Support Division. This position gave him the opportunity to use all of his prior tactical experience to support the patrol officers below in coordinating tactical operations. Many of these operations included perimeter containments. His K-9 experience paid big dividends in the sky over critical incidents where Jack had great success in assisting units to locate suspects on the run. After two years, he switched seats in the helicopter and was selected as a Command Pilot at Air Support Division where he is still assigned.

When it comes to "suspect tactics and perimeter containment" Jack's experience and knowledge certainly give him a unique expertise in this area. He has participated in over 1500 perimeter containments during his career and has seen many successes and failures. He shares this experience with officers across the country instructing on this topic.

Jack has a B.S. in Criminal Justice from Kutztown University of Pennsylvania and is a certified instructor with California Police Officer Standards and Training.

He lives in Santa Clarita, California with his wife Tracy, and children Ian and Megan.

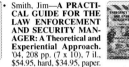

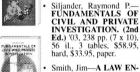